On The Street Where You Live

Volume Three

Sailors, Solicitors, and Stargazers of Early Victoria

On The Street Where You Live

Volume Three

Sailors, Solicitors, and Stargazers of Early Victoria

Danda Humphreys

Heritage House

Copyright © 2001 by Danda Humphreys

National Library of Canada Cataloguing in Publication Data

Humphreys, Danda.
    On the street where you live: sailors, solicitors, and stargazers of early Victoria

    Includes index.
    ISBN 1-894384-31-8 (bound)   ISBN 1-894384-36-9 (paperback)

    1. Street names—British Columbia—Victoria—History. 2. Victoria (B.C.)—Biography. 3. Victoria (B.C.)—History. I. Title.

FC3846.67.H851 2001   971.1'28   C2001-911229-7
F1089.5.V6H851 2001

First edition 2001

All rights reserved. No part of this publication may be reproduced, stored in a retrieval system, or transmitted in any form or by any means—electronic, mechanical, audio recording, or otherwise—without the written permission of the publisher or a photocopying licence from CANCOPY, Toronto, Canada.

Heritage House acknowledges the financial support for our publishing program from the Government of Canada through the Book Publishing Industry Development Program (BPIDP), Canada Council for the Arts, and the British Columbia Arts Council.

Front cover: The Harbour, showing CPR and GT P Steamers. Front flap: Sailing Fleet (top), Oak Bay Drive (bottom). Back cover: Government Street looking South (top), Indian War Canoe Race in the Inner Harbour (bottom).

Cover design and layout by Darlene Nickull
Maps by Brenda Martin
Edited by Audrey McClellan

HERITAGE HOUSE PUBLISHING COMPANY LTD.
Unit #108-17665 66A Avenue, Surrey, B.C. V3S 2A7

Printed in Canada

For J.S. and Lucky and the Beagle Bunch—friends and fellow "street walkers"—may you always stroll on the sunny side!

CONTENTS

Acknowledgements 5
Introduction 7
Cadboro Bay Road: Trail to the fort started at Native village 11
Old Esquimalt Road: First road to the fort 16
Esquimalt Road: A straighter route to Victoria 19
Thetis Lane: Frigate served these shores 22
Race Passage Close: Keepers of the light 25
Walbran Park: A captain of many names 28
Rudlin Street: Skipper in the gold rush 31
Sayward Street: Victoria's first sawmill baron 35
Fan Tan Alley: If those old walls could only talk 38
Powell Street: Victoria's first Canadian-born physician 42
Tiedemann Place: Architect to the colony 46
Trounce Alley: Alley builder trounced obstacles 49
Wilson Street: Clothing capped brothers' success 54
Hibbens Close: Early bookstore set stage for debate 57
Redfern Street: Clockmaker wound up as mayor 60
Goodacre Lake: In the market for meat and vegetables 64
Carroll Street: He served ale in brown jugs 69
Dallas Road: Married the governor's daughter 73
Bushby Street: Early star of the Philharmonic 77
Franklin Terrace: Bachelor brothers made their mark 80
Belmont Road: Governor's brother-in-law and chief justice 83
Young Street: Oh to be young again ... 86
Elliott Street: "A genial, whole-souled gentleman" 89
Pooley Street: Pick and shovel paved his path to parliament 92
Mystic Lane: Who's afraid of Julia Booth? 95
Shakespeare Street: No poetry for the postmaster 98
Pendray Street: The man who cleaned up 102

Rattenbury Place: He had designs on Victoria   106
Maclure Road: The real B.C. Architect   111
Courtney Street: The solicitor and the man of the sea   116
Paul Kane Place: Celebrated artist visited Victoria   120
Sangster Lane: The sad story of James Sangster   124
Denison Road: A dedicated weather man   127
Hastings Street: Stargazer built conservatory   131
Harrison Street: Adventures filled route to Victoria   134
Point Street: There's a story to that Point   137
Medana Street: Medana's farm was James Bay picnic site   143
Earle Street: Adding a little spice to life   147
Prior Street: Practical, pragmatic politician   151
Lotbiniere Avenue: Courteous and non-controversial lieut.-governor   155
Gore Street: Brothers surveyed all before them   158
Service Street: The face at the window   161
Bibliography   175
Index   177
Photo Credits   183
The Author   184

MAPS

This volume contains a complete set of maps identifying location of all streets referenced in the *On The Streets Where You Live* trilogy.

      Location of Streets Included in Volume I   166
      Location of Streets Included in Volume II   169
      Location of Streets Included in Volume III   172

ACKNOWLEDGEMENTS

At the end of the long and winding road through researching and writing a book, it's always a pleasure to acknowledge those who helped along the way. For me, this help has come in many guises—cards, letters, phone calls, e-mails, ideas, personal stories, encouragement, smiles in the supermarket, cheery waves on the street…

People often tell me that my stories have stirred up long-forgotten memories. After reading about Shakespeare Street, one woman called to say that the man it was named after, Noah Shakespeare, was her grandfather. She still remembered visiting him when she was a child, and recalled, "He was a wonderful man!" Another reader chuckled at the chapter about Francis Napier Denison, maintaining he was a better man than a meteorologist: "He was a very nice fellow, but his weather forecasts were always wrong!"

Dozens of people helped me solve the mystery of a missing timepiece. What, I asked, had happened to the clock that once hung over the sidewalk above Charles Redfern's jewellery store? It turned out the clock was moved to a church tower on a farm school near Cowichan Station, where young boys from Britain were evacuated during the Second World War. A former pupil, now in his 90s, recalled how the pain of being separated from his parents and siblings was rendered a little more bearable by being free to run through tall trees and green meadows, so different from the blackouts and bomb shelters of blitz-beleaguered London.

Research is a challenging task, and without the help of archives and museum staff and volunteers it would be far more difficult to fit the pieces of each story puzzle together. My thanks to everyone at the B.C. Provincial Archives, Victoria City Archives, Saanich Municipal Archives, Maritime Museum of British Columbia, Saanich Pioneers Society, Sidney Museum, Sooke Region Museum and Archives, Metchosin School Museum Society, and the Old Cemeteries Society. It has been a privilege and a pleasure to work with you all.

Specific help with family and other histories for this volume came from Dave Parker, Sherri Robinson, and Trevor Wright at Esquimalt Municipal Archives (Esquimalt Road and other Esquimalt stories); Paul Kane V and Suzanne Uher (Paul Kane); Lynn Wright, Maritime Museum of B.C. (*Cadboro*, Captain G.W. Courtenay); Judith Hudson Beattie, Keeper of HBC Archives, and Anne Morton, HBC Archives, Winnipeg, Manitoba (James Sangster, Captain G.W. Courtenay); Nelson McInnis and

Jack Kent (Captain G.W. Courtenay); Don Lovell, University of Victoria Library/Archives (Mystic Spring); Ron Bradley and Ron Weir (Thomas Argyle); Jack Gardner and the Jewish Historical Society (Franklin brothers); Bill Goodacre (Goodacre family).

Special thanks to Peter Salmon, editor of the "Islander," who has supported the series from its 1997 inception and never let me miss a deadline. Also thanks to Jennifer Barr, Maureen Duffus, Chris Hanna, Fred Hook, and Bess Page for help, information, and encouragement.

Hats off to Heritage House for this third book of "street stories." Bouquets to Darlene Nickull for her attractive design. And a special salute to editor Audrey McClellan, who keeps me focused on the road ahead, makes sure I don't turn corners without signalling, and reminds me to look right, left, and right again before I cross the street.

Calling all *Times Colonist* readers! Thanks for spending time with me on Sundays. Who would have thought a simple curiosity about street names would bring us all this far? You've been with me from the start, and as always, this book's for you.

INTRODUCTION

I've always been fascinated by street names. Especially the names of the streets I've lived on. Maybe you, like me, have realized that on the long and sometimes rocky road through life, those street names spell stability. The houses might change, the residents might move on, but the streets—for the most part—stay the same.

Researching stories for these books, I've learned a lot about life in Victoria "in the old days." One thing I've discovered in my travels: if a street name starts with the word "Old," it's well worth exploring. A walk or drive along these half-forgotten byways can yield wonderful surprises. Among the best-known around Victoria are Old West Saanich Road, Old East Road, Old Island Highway, and of course Old Esquimalt Road—the first road to the fort.

In Volumes One and Two of this series we watched as the small fur-trading post established in 1843 on the east side of Victoria's sheltered harbour took on increasing importance. By 1849 it had become the Hudson's Bay Company's northern headquarters. Its future was assured. But what of its past?

For centuries, Native people had lived around the harbour and along the shoreline around the southern tip of Vancouver Island. By the late 1830s, sailing ships were a common sight in the Strait of Juan de Fuca. But when one of those ships sailed right into what we now call Cadboro Bay, the people who lived near the beach there had little idea what the future held in store.

Present-day Cadboro Bay Road follows part of one of the trails used by the Natives during their regular cross-country journeys to find food. By 1843, it also took them to the white man's fort. Approaching the fort from the opposite direction, more Europeans came, tramping along the muddy, three-mile trail from their ship's mooring-point at Esquimalt. A few years later that trail was straightened and widened to make access to the settlement easier.

Many of the first men who followed that trail were hired on contract by the HBC. They sent the money they earned home so that wives and families could brave a long and dangerous sea journey to join them. In Volume One we followed the fortunes of those early arrivals as they left the Company's confines and started on the road to independence. Muddy trails became pioneer pathways as families settled in the densely wooded wildness of Gordon Head, Saanich, Metchosin, and Sooke, clearing the land, cultivating crops, and creating communities.

Introduction

Early architect H.O. Tiedemann (see story page 46) was also an avid illustrator. This "View of Victoria, Vancouver Island, June 13, 1860" gives us Tiedemann's impression of the town two years after his arrival. He sketched looking southeast from Esquimalt. Across the upper harbour from the Songhees (top of page 8), tall trees in the distance mark the extent of the town, south of today's Bay Street. The ravine that preceded today's Johnson Street is visible just to the left of the waterfront buildings. The police barracks (replaced by Tiedemann's courthouse, now the Maritime Museum) are visible alongside the last Fort Victoria buildings. In the image above, beyond the fort, on the horizon, is the Victoria District Church (where the Law Courts now stand on Burdett Avenue). Between the two tall trees right of centre, a wooden bridge spans James Bay, leading to Governor James Douglas's mansion and Tiedemann's own government buildings, known as the Birdcages. Below on page 8, in the distance, are the mountains of the Olympic Peninsula, Washington state. In the early 20th century, the sketch was printed as a distinctive triptych postcard, shown below.

Volume Two took us from the simple homes of those first settlers to the sublime dwellings of the Rithets and the Spencers and the Dunsmuirs. We watched as Victoria's wooden stores and saloons, hastily erected in 1858 to cater to gold-seekers bound for B.C.'s Interior, were replaced by sturdy brick buildings that spelled permanence and prosperity. And we travelled along the railway lines that snaked up the peninsula and out to the western communities, connecting outlying areas with the city's core. Now, for the first time, city dwellers could explore the far reaches of the peninsula and beyond, farmers could more easily transport their produce, and people could shop downtown, where merchants in fine stores displayed a mixture of local products and exotic imports.

In this third volume, the bare bones of Victoria's beginnings, muscled by farmers and men of fortune, are fleshed out with an interesting cast of characters. The people who populate these pages include sailors and saloon-keepers, lawyers, bankers and businessmen, architects and astronomers, doctors, politicians, postmasters, even a poet or two. They come in all shapes and sizes and from all parts of the world. Their stories clothe the city's skeleton, giving it identity and shape. Their names linger on, in the highways, byways, and alleyways of downtown, Old Town, Esquimalt and Victoria West, Oak Bay and Cadboro Bay, James Bay and Fairfield, Tillicum and the Gorge, Colwood, Metchosin and Sooke, Patricia Bay, and points along the coast.

So find yourself a comfy chair. Close your eyes for a moment and imagine the Victoria of days gone by, when these muddy streets and boardwalks were trod by men and women who shaped a simple settlement into the city we know today. Get ready for another peek into the past. And remember—when a road says "old," it usually means that, for the intrepid traveller, a whole new adventure awaits.

CADBORO BAY ROAD

Trail to the fort started at Native village

Several centuries before the first Europeans arrived in what is now called Cadboro Bay, it was the home of a long-forgotten Native tribe. Evidence of their presence here was discovered in the early 1870s by historian James Deans. He wrote a series of newspaper articles comparing the stone mounds near the bay to similar cairns on Beacon Hill. More than 20 years later, scientists confirmed that Cadboro Bay had once served as an important settlement for a Straits-Salish group that vanished without a trace.

What happened to those earlier residents? We'll probably never know. By the late 1830s, when James Douglas first explored this coastline, a group known as the Sungayka, part of the Songhees Nation, was in residence. Sungayka means "snow patches," which may have related to the white sands along the beach or to the real snow patches visible on the mountains to the south and east.

At the centre of the Sungayka settlement was a stockade designed to protect the people from warlike tribes that attacked in the dead of night, killing men and boys and taking women and children as slaves. This structure, which stood near today's Royal Victoria Yacht Club, was not unlike the fort that would shortly take shape some ten miles away on Victoria's harbour.

By 1824 the Sungayka people would have been accustomed to seeing sailing ships in the strait, but it may have been a surprise when one of these ships dropped anchor right on their doorstep, in the bay that would soon bear the vessel's name.

The 72-ton, six-gun brigantine *Cadboro* was the pride of the Pacific. Built for the Hudson's Bay Company (HBC) at Rye, on England's south coast, in 1824, it was 56 feet long with a 17-foot beam. Its first ocean voyage began in the fall of 1826 when it sailed from London with Captain John Swan at the helm, a 35-man crew, and several new HBC employees. Weathering the stormy seas around Cape Horn, *Cadboro* followed the coastline to Oregon Territory, arriving at Fort Vancouver on the Columbia River in June 1827.

Captain Aemilius Simpson, a relative of HBC governor George Simpson, took over as master of the vessel. Later that same year the *Cadboro* set sail for the British Columbia mainland. It was the first boat to sail up the Fraser River, where the tools it carried were used to build the HBC's new post at Fort Langley.

Several months later, with that mission complete, *Cadboro* returned to Fort Vancouver, only to learn of a tragedy. A band of Clallam

Cattle Point, on Cadboro Bay, was the landing site for cattle brought from the mainland for delivery to Uplands and other farms.

Indians from the Strait of Juan de Fuca had attacked and killed a group of HBC men. The *Cadboro* anchored off the Clallam village, and when the murderers refused to surrender, the crew opened fire. Several Indians were killed, and this proved to be the last time anyone attacked the white men in this area.

A decade later, Captain William Brotchie brought James Douglas aboard the *Cadboro* to the southern tip of Vancouver Island. Douglas explored the coastline south from Sooke, looking for a suitable site for a fort. Each harbour had its merits, he reported, but the port of Camosack, or Camosun, had more advantages than most. It was safe and accessible, with an "abundance of timber for home consumption and exploitation."

As Fort Victoria took shape on the Inner Harbour and HBC activities expanded up-Island, the *Cadboro*'s role expanded along with

Top left: In the early 1900s there were few dwellings on the waterfront where Natives once camped. Nestled among sheltering trees were buildings on land belonging to the area's first settlers—Michael Finnerty, John Sinclair, Edwin Hobbs, and Benjamin Evans

Built in Rye, England, and purchased for the Pacific northwest coast fur trade in 1826, the Cadboro *(or* Cadborough, *as it was originally named) arrived on this coast a year later (bottom left). In 1837, when James Douglas started serious exploration of southern Vancouver Island, it was Captain William Brotchie who brought the vessel here. Five years later she sailed into what we now call Cadboro Bay. The* Cadboro *was wrecked in Puget Sound in October 1860.*

In 1864, the Hotel Willows stood near the corner of what are now Cadboro Bay and Eastdowne roads.

them. In 1850, now captained by James Sangster, it carried the first shipment of coal from Newcastle Island, near Nanaimo, to Victoria Harbour.

That same year the *Cadboro* fell foul of the law south of the border. First the crew was accused of harbouring ten American soldiers who had deserted to Victoria. Peter Skene Ogden, the chief factor at Fort Vancouver, expressed his dismay that the HBC would "connive at such a disgraceful act." A few days later the *Cadboro* was in trouble again when she became the first HBC ship to be seized by U.S. revenue officials. The charge: non-payment of duty to the United States government for goods landed in Oregon Territory. Eventually the HBC agreed to pay the disputed monies, and the *Cadboro* was free to continue its regular duties.

For almost two decades the *Cadboro* plied the waters along this coastline, carrying furs and oil from Nootka Sound to Fort Vancouver. However in 1857, HBC records show the *Cadboro* was "laid up in harbour, not having been required for any service since last year," and by the time gold was discovered on the Fraser River in 1858, the *Cadboro* was decidedly the worse for wear.

Two years later it was sold at auction to a

Captain Howard for $340 and began a new career transporting coal and lumber between Victoria and neighbouring ports. On October 6, 1860, laden with lumber, the ship was caught in a gale a few miles from Port Angeles, sprang a leak, and started to sink. The captain beached it safely, but before long the *Cadboro* was gone, its gallant old hull battered to pieces by the relentless waves.

Back at Cadboro Bay, the scene was changing. Once the Hudson's Bay fort was established on the east side of Victoria's inner harbour in 1843, the Songhees people started to leave the shores of Cadboro Bay for longer periods. This had traditionally been their centre of operations, but now they were spending more time around the fort.

In those days they travelled west across the countryside via a series of trails that crossed oak-studded meadows and cedar-filled swamps until they reached the harbour. Today we call the eastern part of that historic route Cadboro Bay Road.

First road to the fort

Today's Esquimalt Road winds from the Inner Harbour through a busy suburb west of Victoria's city centre, but in the 1840s Esquimalt was a quieter, more peaceful place. Once it was near the site of an Indian village, where Native people celebrated the passing of the seasons in time-honoured ways. Once, the only sounds that echoed here were the footfalls of the first European arrivals heading for the Hudson's Bay Company fort along a trail that we now call Old Esquimalt Road.

At the west end of this trail in the late 1840s, ships carrying HBC workers dropped anchor in a sheltered bay that once had a Spanish name—Puerto de Cordova. It was navigator Manuel Quimper's first mate, Gonzalo de Lopez de Haro, who in 1790 named the harbour after the 46th viceroy of New Spain. Two years later, when Galiano and Valdes anchored here, Galiano noted the abundance of wild roses. "The port of Cordova," he wrote in his journal, "is beautiful."

In 1842, however, James Douglas chose to call the harbour by its original Native name, which he wrote as "Is-whoy-malth." The translation—"place of gradually shoaling waters"—probably refers to the movement of the water where a fast-running stream (Millstream) emptied into the harbour at its northern end.

Douglas thought this harbour one of the best on the coast, but reported that, in his opinion, it wasn't fit for a fort: "I did not see one level spot clear of trees of sufficient extent to build a large fort upon. There is in fact no clear land within a quarter of a mile of the harbour." Instead, he chose to build the fort at the nearby Port of Camosack, on a level clearing.

Not long afterwards, a surveying team of Royal Engineers pooh-poohed his choice. Esquimalt Harbour, they declared, was far superior. But it was too late. Douglas's mind was made up. Esquimalt, he had decided, was destined for bigger and better things.

In 1849 the HBC negotiated with Great Britain a seven-shillings-a-year lease for the whole of Vancouver Island and put Douglas in charge of it. He earmarked Esquimalt for development on behalf of the Puget Sound Agricultural Company. Before long, three huge farms covered most of the area. Bailiffs were hired to manage the farms. Workers were hired in Britain to run the farms and help develop a settlement around the fort. Company ships brought them to Victoria by way of Esquimalt.

R.F. Britten painted this 1862 view of Esquimalt Harbour and HMC Topaze *(note the original spelling, unlike today's Topaz-without-an-e Avenue).*

Sailors, being a hardy lot, were undaunted by having to follow the rocky coastline to the fort in an Indian canoe or small boat. But it was a dangerous exercise, even for experienced seafarers, and drownings were not infrequent. Non-sailing settlers arriving from afar, with high hopes and even higher expectations, were less inclined to risk their lives in the rock-studded, kelp-ridden waters. Instead, they chose to walk to their new home.

The narrow, winding trail—formed by animals, then followed by humans—was three miles long. It was rough, uneven, and muddy most of the year. A miserable journey for men, it was many times worse for their long-skirted wives, often with children in tow. And so in 1852, sailors from HMS *Thetis* hacked and slashed their way through seemingly impenetrable forest and built the first official road to the fort. They started at what is now the corner of Esquimalt and Admirals, then moved east along the peninsula. To the north, the simple track that became Admirals Road led to Kenneth McKenzie's Craigflower Farm.

Just east of Admirals, swampland sent the sailors scurrying up a steep incline (Park Terrace) to avoid it. Cutting through Donald Macaulay's Viewfield Farm, they climbed steadily, clearing a path along the rocky ridge below another hill (Rock Heights). From here, it was a straight run east (across Lampson), then over to join (at Wilson and Bay) the trail that ran from Craigflower through Thomas Skinner's Constance Cove Farm. Eventually they reached the water's edge, where a wooden bridge crossed the upper harbour.

Wooden buildings once clustered around the landing on the Esquimalt waterfront where many a traveller was relieved to again set foot on British soil. Old Esquimalt Village has long since been swallowed up by the dockyard.

The tiny settlement on Esquimalt Harbour grew, spreading swiftly along either side of the road the sailors had built. Starting in April 1858, thousands of gold miners sailed in from the south and headed for the city, en route to the Fraser River. Royal Navy ships anchored at Royal Roads, ready to protect the British subjects, and in 1865, Esquimalt was finally recognized as a permanent naval base.

By that time a more direct route had been created—now called Esquimalt Road—and some interesting people eventually lived, loved, and laboured along the way.

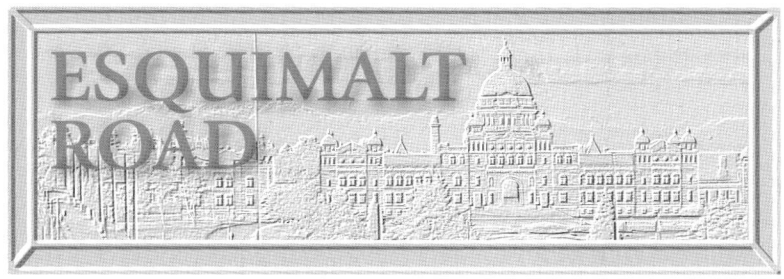

A straighter route to Victoria

Gold fever spurred the growth of the village that was the landing place for Victoria's newest arrivals. Some were seasoned gold miners. Some were novices, ready to work hard and reap the anticipated rewards. Others were "drifters" who—largely unprepared and with little respect for the law—were anxious to make money fast, and not necessarily through the fruit of their own labours.

The ships that brought these people to Vancouver Island's shores did not discriminate between them. One and all, they followed the same route to Victoria, along the trail created by the men of the *Thetis* some five years before. More bodies meant more business. Astute local merchants quickly built warehouses, stores, hotels, and saloons to soothe the weary along the way. But what they really needed was a better road to Victoria.

By the mid-1860s, all three Puget Sound Agricultural Company farms—none of which, for one reason or another, had lived up to PSAC's expectations—were gone. The land was subdivided and sold, and in 1865 a new access route was driven right through the middle of what had once been Viewfield Farm.

Former bailiff Donald Macaulay, who was still in the area, must have been amazed to see what short work the road builders made of the land he had struggled so hard to clear some fifteen years before. Once again, it was the Navy to the rescue. Starting just east of Admirals Road, a team from the *Cleo* led by Charles (later Lord Charles) Beresford ignored the steep hill up to the ridge on their left. Instead, they pressed straight on through the virgin forest toward Victoria. Following that same route today, we see street names that remind us of those early times. Many reflect Esquimalt's naval heritage. Nelson, Grenville, Lyall, Craddock, Beatty, Sturdee, Naden, Grafton, Constance, Juno, Lampson, and Head are just a few that honour Navy men and ships.

Tired and thirsty travellers disembarking at Esquimalt didn't have far to go for a tipple. John Day's Esquimalt Hotel—also known as the Bucket of Blood—was right at the end of Wharf Street (later renamed Pioneer Street, then swallowed up by the dockyard). From there it was a long haul around the base of Signal Hill, past the first location of St. Paul's Anglican Church, and up a steep slope to May Simpson's Coach and Horses (later the chief and petty officers' mess). A man could be forgiven for needing to whet his whistle again—if not here, then just up the road at Mrs. Jacques's Sailor's

This 1880s view from Admirals Road shows the wharf at Plumper Bay.

Rest (originally the Methodist Soldiers and Sailors Home; now the Tudor House). If yours was a thirst that could not be slaked on the journey east, there was always the Halfway House.

James and Elizabeth Bland built their wooden roadhouse and brewery halfway from Esquimalt to Victoria in 1860. Designed to serve two-legged customers, it was also home for a short while to several of the four-legged variety—camels destined for freight-carrying in the Cariboo gold fields. Once there were three other saloons between this roadhouse and Rock Bay. However, the Blands probably never dreamed that theirs would be the only one still serving thirsty patrons—but no camels—to this day.

Down near the foot of Lampson Street (named after the *Lady Lampson*), Munro Street reminds us of Alexander Munro, accountant and general manager of the Puget Sound Agricultural Company, which owned Viewfield Farm. South of Munro and east of Lampson, where Viewfield's rockiest section dropped down to the water, there was, in later years, an earthwork battery. Fort Macaulay, like Fort Rodd Hill and Victoria Battery on Dallas Road near Battery Street, were links in a chain of fortifications built along this coast in 1878 to help protect the British fleet from Russian attack. Fortunately, they were never needed.

Not far from where Head Street (named for the *Lady Head*) crosses Esquimalt, at West Bay, lived the Jacobsons. Victor was Finnish, a sea captain who became wealthy courtesy of the seal industry. He and his wife Minnie lived in the house that still stands next to Victor Jacobson Park, overlooking the marina. On the marina's south side, Work Point Barracks—named for HBC chief factor John Work and now part of CFB Esquimalt—was built as an army base in 1887.

In 1865, Beresford's Esquimalt Road building crew eventually reached the Inner Harbour through land that had for centuries been home to the Songhees people. Now the view across the water was quite different from when Old Esquimalt Road had been built some thirteen years before. Where the HBC settlement once stood was now a thriving commercial centre. Victoria was a newly incorporated city. But new or old, Esquimalt Road would always be remembered as the first road to the fort.

Not long after the turn of the century, these sailors marched along Esquimalt Road to Victoria to celebrate King Edward VII's birthday. As they approach Canteen Road, headed up the hill toward Nelson Street, a gable belonging to St. Paul's Church (in its second location) can be seen at upper right. A streetcar track runs along the left side of the road. On the right, a trestle carries walkers high above the swamp.

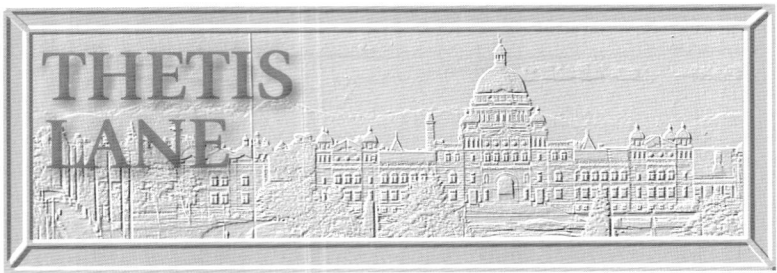

Frigate served these shores

Tucked between Beacon and Niagara streets in James Bay is a short lane that reminds us of some brave sailors. Thetis Lane honours the vessel whose men left their mark on Victoria a century and a half ago. And it reminds us that Vancouver Island and the northwest coast were just one stop on this ship's voyage of adventure.

What's in a name? In Greek mythology, Thetis was the mother of Achilles. To the Latin poets, Thetis simply meant "sea." The *Thetis* that sailed to Vancouver Island's shores was the eighth ship to bear the name. Described as a 36-gun sailing frigate, fifth rate, it was designed in England by members of the School of Naval Architecture established in Portsmouth Dockyard.

Built in Devonport Dockyard, the *Thetis* was launched in August 1846. Newspaper reports of the time stated that it "instantly glided into her native element in beautiful style . . . as fine a frigate as ever swam." By December it was ready for the sea. On New Year's Eve, 1846, the ship sailed for Lisbon. Portugal was in a state of civil war. Europe was in turmoil. The *Thetis* spent two years in the Mediterranean, at Messina, Sicily, Naples, Genoa, Corfu, Malta, and the Dardanelles, her crew providing protection for British residents and offering what help they could.

This first commission completed, the *Thetis* returned to England's Plymouth Sound in June 1850. There, the frigate prepared for another adventure—one that would eventually bring it to the northwest coast.

For this journey the *Thetis* was to be under the command of Captain Augustus Kuper. Born in 1809, the son of a chaplain, Kuper joined the navy at the age of 15 and had been promoted to lieutenant at the age of 22. He served in Australia and India before commissioning the *Thetis* for foreign service.

His plans seemed not to inspire much interest. After two weeks, only 150 men—less than half the number needed—had joined the crew. Finally, in October, there was a full crew and the ship was ready to sail. First port of call was Madeira, and then Rio in late December. Here the crew was plagued by yellow fever. Several died. In March 1851, fever-free at last, the *Thetis* sailed for Bahia and Montevideo. Two months later it was ordered to the Pacific Station.

The *Thetis* arrived at Valparaiso in mid-August and was joined there by Acting Lieutenant John Moresby, previously gunnery mate on the *Amphitrite* and son of Rear Admiral Fairfax Moresby, commander-in-chief of the Pacific Station. After several months at the

The Royal Navy frigate Thetis *spent only eight months in these waters, but her name and the road-building efforts of her crew live on in our history.*

station, the *Thetis* was ordered north to investigate news of a gold find on Queen Charlotte's Island (before the discovery of Skidegate Channel, it was believed this group of islands was one large land mass), named after the wife of England's King George III.

Kuper and his crew sailed into the Strait of Juan de Fuca on Queen Victoria's birthday, May 24, 1852, and anchored at Esquimalt. Kuper and Moresby went by boat along the coastline to visit Governor James Douglas at Fort Victoria. One of their ship's predecessors had something in common with Douglas. The sixth *Thetis*, a Dutch-owned gun ship, was captured at Demerara, British Guiana, in 1796, just seven years before James Douglas was born there.

Following Douglas's instructions, the *Thetis* sailed to Queen Charlotte's Island, where an HBC officer was waiting to pilot them into Gold Harbour. They found that the small amount of gold there was difficult to extract in any quantity, and the "gold rush" quickly expired. After exploring Port Kuper and the nearby lakes, which Kuper named after his young lieutenant, the *Thetis* returned to Esquimalt.

There was much travel to and from the fort, but the sea journey was not without its hazards, and there were several mishaps along the way. Eventually, when an officer and two men became entangled in kelp and drowned after their boat

This view of the bridge between Thetis and Kuper islands was taken in the 1920s. Captain Augustus Leopold Kuper, RN, commander of the Thetis, *was on this station from 1851 to 1853.*

capsized, fellow crew members took up axes and cut the route through the forest that we now call Old Esquimalt Road.

In November 1852, the *Thetis* was in Esquimalt Harbour when news came of the murder near the fort of a young HBC shepherd, Peter Brown. At Douglas's request, Kuper and his crew accompanied the *Beaver* to Cowichan, where the Native perpetrators of the crime were apprehended, tried, and hanged.

Once more, the *Thetis* returned to Esquimalt. By 1853 it was ready to move on. Sailing for England via San Francisco, Mazatlan, Panama, Valparaiso, and Rio, the ship arrived in Plymouth in January 1854. That same year it was traded to Prussia in return for two iron paddlewheelers.

In eight short months here, the *Thetis* made quite an impression on the people of Victoria, particularly the local cricket team, which was beaten hollow by Moresby and his men during Vancouver Island's first cricket match at Beacon Hill.

Victoria's Maritime Museum contains much information on the journeys of this famous frigate. Thetis Lane in James Bay, Thetis Crescent and Kuper Avenue in Colwood, Moresby Street in Esquimalt, Moresby Park Terrace in North Saanich, Thetis Island, and Thetis Cove in Esquimalt Harbour, Port Kuper, Kuper Island, and Moresby Island and Passage all remind us of the men who helped protect us from danger in days gone by.

Keepers of the light

The cairn in Highrock Park says it's eleven miles from Esquimalt to Race Rocks, but from Mount Matheson's Race Passage Close it's just a hop, skip, and a jump. The view from here, out over Becher Bay to Race Rocks, is magnificent. The men of the *Thetis* would have welcomed such a sight. But they were a few years too soon. The lighthouse that alerted sailors to danger didn't flash its warning until 1860—long after the *Thetis* had gone.

Officers of the Hudson's Bay Company named Race Rocks in 1842. Four years later, Henry Kellett, captain of the surveying vessel HMS *Herald*, declared the name of the small rocky island to be appropriate for, as he observed, the tide literally raced around it.

These were dangerous waters for wooden sailing ships, which started visiting the area in ever-increasing numbers. Navigational aids would surely help. In 1859 a group of men including Captain Richards of the *Plumper*; Captain Fulford of the *Ganges*; Captain Mouat of the HBC steamer *Otter*; Captain Cooper, harbour master for British Columbia; and Captain Nagle, harbour master for Vancouver Island, along with surveyor-general Joseph Pemberton, selected sites for two lighthouses. One was on Fisgard Island in Esquimalt Harbour; the other, eleven miles away at Race Rocks.

The British government set aside 7,000 pounds sterling for the project. Fisgard Light went into operation December 1, 1860. Just over three weeks later, Race Rocks followed suit.

Not for nothing did Kellett describe these rocks as a "dangerous group." Riptides, dangerous currents, and fog in the vicinity took their toll of seagoing vessels long before the lighthouse was built, and would continue to do so for decades to come. But perhaps the most tragic accident of all happened almost five years to the day after Race Rocks first shone its warning light.

On December 24, 1865, lightkeeper George Davies' sister, brother-in-law, and three male friends sailed out to the station to celebrate Christmas Day. Their boat was caught in a tide rip and capsized. One of its occupants managed to cling to the sailboat and drifted within twenty feet of land, but no one could reach him. The station's lifeboat had been lost in a recent storm, and amazingly, there was no rope or lifebuoy. In full view of the horrified friends and relatives who waited on the rock to greet them, all of the sailboat's passengers drowned. Lightkeeper Davies was overcome with grief. Two years later, he too was dead.

Race Rocks lighthouse in the 1870s.

Pictured with Thomas and Ellen Argyle in the 1870s are the six children born at Race Rocks (from left): Anne (Molly), baby Jenny, Grace standing behind young Maude, Frederick (leaning on Thomas's knee), and Louisa.

Second keeper of the light was Thomas Argyle, who was born in Birmingham, England, in 1838. In 1858 he joined the Royal Engineers and was one of a specially selected group chosen for duties in the new colony across the sea. In April 1859 he sailed into Esquimalt Harbour on his way to the mainland, little dreaming that in a few short years he would return to these shores for good.

While based at Sapperton, the men of Argyle's Royal Engineers detachment surveyed towns, constructed roads, and built bridges all through the Fraser Valley. They designed the province's first postage stamp, New Westminster's first English churches, and a coat-of-arms for B.C.

In October 1863, after its obligatory five years' service to the Crown, the detachment disbanded. Argyle elected to stay in B.C. and started a new business. Two months later, an announcement in the local newspaper declared that Thomas Argyle, gunsmith and general jobbing smith, had set up an office on Front Street where he was "prepared to execute with neatness and despatch all kinds of work in the above lines" and vowed to clean and keep in good repair rifles, fowling pieces, and pistols "on the most reasonable terms."

Earlier that same year, Argyle had married Mary Ellen Tufts, whose ancestors from Norfolk, England, sailed to America on the *Mayflower*. For several generations the Tufts had lived in Halifax, Nova Scotia, where Ellen was born. A deceptively fragile-looking woman, she was in fact brave, strong, and adventurous for her time. This

Fisgard lighthouse protected the entrance to Esquimalt Harbour and warned sailors of the dangerous rocks near Royal Roads.

strength would serve her well in the years to come.

Thomas and Ellen had three children—Albert, Helen, and Thomas Jr.—by 1867, when Argyle was appointed chief keeper of the lighthouse at Race Rocks. Six more children were born there. Life with such a large family was never dull, and a lighthouse-keeper is never short of work. In his spare time, Thomas Sr. liked to swim and dive. It's said that he found many a gold sovereign among the wreckage of ships that had come to grief around Race Rocks. He was also known for his life-saving efforts.

One day in 1877 those efforts, although well intentioned, were apparently misguided. Seeing two men clinging to a rough raft formed from two lashed-together logs, Argyle hurried to rescue and revive them ... only to discover that they were deserters from HMS *Shah*. Argyle, the good Samaritan, was charged with aiding and abetting the miscreants and was fined $100. The charges were later dropped.

Starting in 1883, Argyle was plagued by ill health and applied for medical leaves of absence several times over the next few years. In March 1888 he retired, moved his wife and younger children to the Rocky Point acreage he had bought some years earlier, and became a farmer. Oldest son Albert took over as keeper of the light. It should have been a happy time, but later that year the family was rocked with grief when Thomas Jr. drowned in a boating accident near the rocks.

The senior Argyles sold the Rocky Point farm in 1912 and moved to Victoria. They lived on Dunedin Street, and Thomas apparently also owned a house where the University of Victoria campus is today. In 1919 he died, aged 81, at his Dunedin Street home. Ellen moved to Burnaby and lived with oldest daughter Helen until she too died, in 1923, at the age of 87. Helen is buried with her parents in Ross Bay Cemetery. Argyle Avenue and Place remind us of her father, enterprising former keeper of the Race Rocks light.

A captain of many names

*I*f you've ever gazed across the Strait of Juan de Fuca from Gonzales Hill, you've been close to a small park named after one of the province's most memorable mariners. Captain John Thomas Walbran sailed extensively in these waters, and in his later years he published a book recording the historical origin of names around British Columbia's coastline.

When Walbran was born in Yorkshire, England, in 1848, Queen Victoria had been on the throne for eleven years. The fort named in her honour on the southern tip of Vancouver Island was still a sleepy Hudson's Bay Company post. The settlement had but one "street"—a trail that led from the fort's east gate through forest, marsh, and meadow to Cadboro Bay. Its future chief factor and later governor, James Douglas, was still based at Fort Vancouver on the Columbia River in the Oregon Territory.

In the mid-1850s, while Walbran was attending Ripon Grammar School in Yorkshire, Fort Victoria was still a fur trading post, surrounded by a few farms. Then came the Fraser River gold rush. By the time Walbran was training for sea service on HM school frigate *Conway* in 1862, Victoria was incorporated as a city. When he became a master mariner in 1881, Victoria was the capital of British Columbia, the colony of B.C. had entered Confederation, and Sir James Douglas, KGB, was dead.

Walbran's career as a mariner progressed steadily. By 1888 he was working for the Canadian Pacific Navigation Company, and within two years was serving as captain of the SS *Danube*. Joining the Marine and Fisheries service in May 1891, he went to Paisley in Scotland to attend the building of the Canadian Government steamship *Quadra*. He captained the new vessel to this coast, and worked for the provincial lighthouse, buoy, and fisheries service for the next twelve years.

Walbran's duties took him up, down, and around the

Captain John Walbran

Captain Charles William Barkley and his seventeen-year-old bride Frances were newlyweds when they first arrived in Nitinat, renamed Barkley Sound by Captain Barkley in 1787.

coast, examining, inspecting, servicing, reporting. He sailed into almost every bay, explored every inlet. Along the way he amassed a vast knowledge of seafarers and seafaring stories, which he passed on to an enthralled public through a lecture series.

In 1901 he entertained the Natural History Society with the tale of Captain Charles William Barkley, who in 1786 had sailed to these shores with his seventeen-year-old wife Frances. Following a route from Belgium around Cape Horn, their ship *Imperial Eagle* called in at the Sandwich Islands (Hawaii) for provisions, then headed for Nootka Sound. Recent severe storms had left the area bereft of other ships. Barkley was able to buy a large quantity of sea otter skins from Indian traders and promptly sailed with them to China, India, and a lifetime of maritime adventures.

Blessed with a love of words and a fascination for history, Walbran used his time wisely. It intrigued him to note that in his travels he was following the routes taken by the great eighteenth-century British and Spanish navigators, men with names like Cook, Cordova, Vancouver, Quadra, Quimper, Galiano. By the time he retired from government service in 1903, he had gathered enough information to form the basis for his most enterprising and enduring project—a study of B.C. coastal names.

Walbran and his family were now living in James Bay, on the corner of Dallas and Menzies streets, where his house stands to this day. In the relative peacefulness of turn-of-the-century Victoria, it was the perfect location for the retired mariner to concentrate on research and writing, close to the ocean he loved so well.

In 1906 he ventured for the first time to make public mention of his new project and started to scour public libraries and private collections for additional information. When *British Columbia Coast Names: Their origin and history* was published in 1909, its list of acknowledgements included, among others, James Bay neighbours Dr. J.S. Helmcken, Bishop Edward Cridge, and Senator W.J. Macdonald.

In his introduction to the 1971 reprint version of the book, historian G.P.V. Akrigg points out the impressive array of Walbran's printed and manuscript sources, ranging from Captain George Vancouver's *Voyage of Discovery* to Swanton's *Haida Texts*, and from the *Nautical Magazine* and *Naval Chronicle* to the HBC's early Nanaimo and Fort Simpson posts' journals. For personal recollections, Walbran turned to people like Thomas Lowe, who had been present at the founding of Fort Victoria, and Captain G.H. Inskip, RN, who had skippered HMS *Virago* during her 1850s coastal surveys. In all, 65 individuals were credited with contributing information.

Pictured on the Dallas Road cliffs with friends, Anne Walbran is at left. Daughter Florence is wearing the white dress. This view looks along Dallas Road toward Ogden Point.

To this day, Walbran's book makes for fascinating reading. It is much more than just a historical directory of place names. Providing far more detail than one might expect in such a document, it is almost a history in itself, an alphabetized account of the West Coast's earliest beginnings and the people who forged them. Akrigg describes it best: "… an amazing grab-bag of history, biography and anecdote … a splendid book in which to browse."

When Walbran's book was published in 1909, Victoria was a very different city from the one he had first sailed to some twenty years before. Now Canadian Pacific's ocean-going Empress liners docked farther west along Dallas Road, at R.P. Rithet's wharves. Carriages took passengers across the James Bay peninsula to the splendid Inner Harbour, with its majestic Legislative Buildings and elegant Empress Hotel. The Golden Anniversary of Victoria's settlement had come and gone, and Queen Victoria along with it.

Sadly, Walbran did not have long to enjoy his retirement. He died at St. Joseph's Hospital at the age of 64 in March 1913, six years after his wife Anne. His wife and daughters are commemorated by Cape Anne, Florence Island, and Ethel Island. Walbran himself is remembered in Walbran Island, Rock, and Point and by that lofty patch of parkland up on Gonzales Hill.

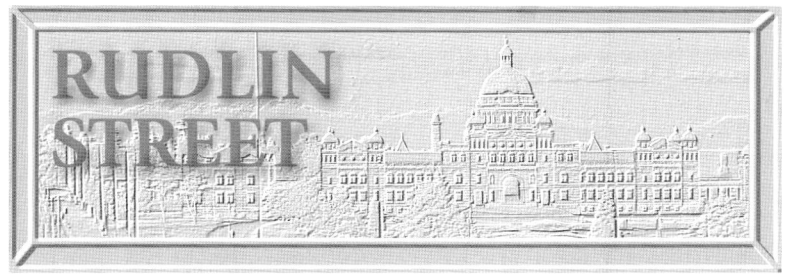

Skipper in the gold rush

Almost a full page in Captain John Walbran's *British Columbia Coast Names* is devoted to the exploits of another well-known sailor, Captain George Rudlin.

Rudlin was born in Essex, England, in 1836. By 1848, the year of Captain Walbran's birth, Rudlin was already at sea, working on a fishing boat. In 1854, while Walbran was in grammar school in Yorkshire, Rudlin was serving in the Crimean War on Her Majesty's transport steamship *Victoria*. It was an exciting time for the eighteen-year-old sailor. While he was at Balaclava in November 1854, there was a fierce storm with heavy gales. Ships were shattered and many lives were lost. Rudlin was luckier than most; he lived to tell the tale.

He arrived on this coast in 1856, sailing first from Valparaiso up to San Francisco. Less than a decade after the gold rush had brought hundreds of gold-seekers to California, San Francisco still had an unsophisticated, small-town feeling. But it was pleasant enough, and Rudlin might have stayed there had not news of another gold find reached him. Along with hundreds of others, he made his way north. The overland trek took time and money, and he didn't reach Esquimalt aboard the *Cotumbia* until 1859.

Resisting the urge to become swept along in the fevered flow of humanity headed for the Fraser River, Rudlin opted to stay in Victoria. A few months later he settled on Discovery Island, off Oak Bay, named after the ship captained by George Vancouver during his 1790s exploration of these shores. Rudlin and another fellow started a logging operation on the island. Rudlin bought the schooner *Circus*, renamed it *Discovery*, and used it to carry coal and lumber up and down the coast.

Five years later, Rudlin took command of the *Black Diamond*, which carried coal between Nanaimo and Victoria, then captained the *Emma* and the *Grappler*. He became part owner of a towing and

Captain George Rudlin

In 1898 the Canadian Pacific Navigation Company steamship Islander *carried gold-seekers to the Klondike.*

transportation company that acquired the *Beaver* from the HBC. Rudlin was the paddle steamer's captain for almost three years. Over the years he was master of many ships with wonderful names like *Wilson G Hunt, Cariboo Fly,* and *Princess Louise.* Decades later, Emily Carr would write about the sights her father and sisters had seen as the *Princess Louise* carried them on an incredible journey up the coast of Vancouver Island.

Somewhere in the middle of all these adventures, Rudlin found time to marry. His wife was the sister-in-law of the proprietor of his favourite Victoria watering hole—the Royal Hotel. Sophia Hill, born in Birmingham, England, in 1830, had travelled to Victoria to join her sister and her husband. She was a capable woman who helped her sister manage the Royal during its owner's frequent forays to the Interior in search of gold. It was Sophia who tended Rudlin when he arrived at the hotel one day with an injured arm, and it was Sophia who stole his heart.

They were married in 1868 and settled in a home Rudlin had built for them on the south side of Pandora, not far from Chambers Street, still recognized in those days as the unofficial eastern boundary of the town. Their house was surrounded by a garden and orchards, which Sophia—childless and with energy to spare—lovingly tended during her husband's long absences.

Through the '80s and '90s, Rudlin captained several Canadian Pacific Navigation Company (CPNC) steamships, including the *R P Rithet, Yosemite, Western Slope, Islander,* and *Charmer.* It was aboard the *Islander* that Rudlin and his employer, CPNC owner Captain John Irving, ran afoul of the law. The Glasgow-built, steel-hulled *Islander* was the finest vessel on this coast when it sailed here in 1888. Plying the Victoria–Vancouver route in record time, it was the

The SS Charmer, *arriving at the dock in Nanaimo, B.C., was one of many mail and passenger ships that once served this coast.*

Captain Rudlin and the crew of the Charmer.

In 1905 the Princess Victoria, *star of the Canadian Pacific fleet, sailed into a Victoria Harbour devoid of high-rises and hotels. At left is Laurel Point. Esquimalt is on the right. The Ship Point docks are in the foreground.*

unchallenged star of Irving's fleet. It was also the centre of a dispute when, during Victoria's smallpox scare, it attempted to deliver a routine cargo of mail and passengers to the CPNC dock in Vancouver. Newly incorporated as a city, Vancouver now boasted a medical officer and a flourishing police force that successfully blocked the *Islander*'s access to the wharf. The captain outwitted them and landed his precious cargo farther east, at Moodyville.

As the century came to a close, CPNC was taken over by the Canadian Pacific Railway Company. A new Victoria–Vancouver–Seattle service was planned, and a new, sleeker, faster ship was ordered from England. Soon after the *Princess Victoria* arrived in Victoria in March 1903, CP announced that the new vessel would be under the command of Captain George Rudlin.

It was an honour and a challenge, and Rudlin rose to meet it. He would not enjoy it for long. Just one month after taking the *Princess Victoria*'s helm, he suffered a heart attack and died while ashore in Vancouver. He was only 67 years old, a genial, popular soul who would be sorely missed. He was buried at Ross Bay Cemetery, joined a decade later by Sophia.

The ships he commanded are long since gone. Rudlin Bay, on Discovery Island, and Fernwood's Rudlin Street are rare reminders of the sea captain who sailed these waters a century ago.

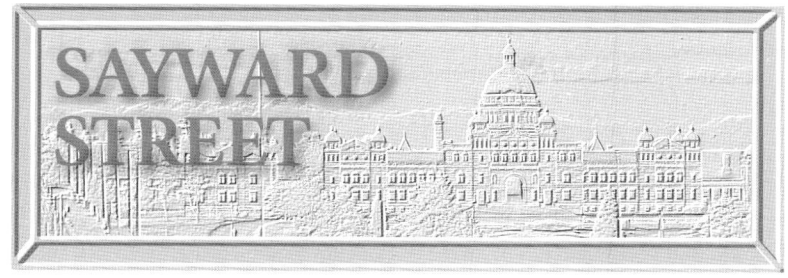

Victoria's first sawmill baron

Captain George Rudlin's first cargo of lumber, brought from Puget Sound aboard *Discovery* in 1860, was delivered to W.P. Sayward's yard on Wharf Street.

William Parson Sayward was born to English parents near Thomastown, Maine, in 1818. As a boy, working hard on the farm and in the forest surrounding his home, he learned the skills that would serve him well many years later in a land far away. Leaving school at sixteen, he apprenticed as a house carpenter, working his way up through carpentering to architect, contractor, and builder.

In the late 1830s he travelled down the Atlantic coast seeking work and ended up in Key West, Florida. There he built houses, factories, and a church until 1849, when news came that gold had been discovered in California. He followed others across the gulf and over the Isthmus of Panama.

He sailed up the West Coast to San Francisco, arriving in midsummer. With three others, he started a bakery and made money supplying the hungry gold miners. When the gold rush slowed to a trickle, he entered the lumber trade. Once again his timing was perfect; the city was growing fast and business was brisk.

Just about the time the town started to encroach on the shoreline in front of his lumberyard, news came of another gold find, on the Fraser River. Sayward sold up and sailed north, arriving at Esquimalt in the early summer of 1858 with hundreds of men who were eager to dig for gold. Sayward's sights, however, were set on more practical activities; he realized that, like San Francisco before it, Victoria was about to boom, and that a steady supply of lumber would be needed.

Interestingly, although beautiful tall trees surrounded the town, no one had the expertise to cut and mill them. Redwood was imported from California and red oak was imported from England. Sayward quickly opened a lumberyard on Wharf Street at the foot of Courtney, where the old Customs House stands today. He imported lumber from a Puget Sound mill, which arrived aboard Captain George Rudlin's *Discovery*, then started towing lumber from Sam Shepard's mill at Mill Bay on Saanich Inlet.

In 1861 he bought Shepard's mill, and in 1878 he established his own mill just a short distance north of Victoria's city centre, at the north end of Store Street. Before long, Rock Bay Saw Mills was dealing exclusively with native lumber—Douglas fir and cedar from the east

William Parson Sayward opened Victoria's first commercial sawmill. In the early 1890s, W.P. Sayward's Rock Bay Saw Mills, at the north end of Store Street, employed more than 100 men and ran round the clock.

coast of Vancouver Island.

In 1861, the same year he acquired Shepard's mill, Sayward married. His wife, Ann, was the widow of James Chambers, after whom Chambers Street is named. She lived with her young son Walter on View Street west of Blanshard, where a parkade stands today. Sayward carefully chose native woods for the home he built for his new family on Collinson Street.

"Woodvine Cottage" stood on property that stretched through to McClure Street. In front of the house a great elderberry tree graced the lawn that sloped down to Collinson. Barns, stables, a creamery, and a root house identified "Woodvine Cottage" as a farm. Cows and horses grazed in the fields to the west of the house. In those days the town limits were Chambers Street, so the 600 block of Collinson Street was almost out in the country. The Saywards' son Joseph was born there in 1862.

The Saywards were sociable souls, and Ann was a motherly sort. Her parlour was the setting for several wedding ceremonies. One celebrated the union of Samuel Nesbitt, who like Sayward had made money as a baker, and his eighteen-year-old bride-ship bride, Jane Anne Saunders.

As Victoria grew from an HBC settlement into a thriving city, W.P. did well. The decades went by and in 1889 his mills, lumber camps, scows, and a steamer employed a total of 50 workers. By 1891 the Rock Bay mill was running continuously, cutting from 60,000 to 70,000 feet of lumber per day. Huge log booms filled Rock Bay. The total number of employees now exceeded 130.

William Sayward's son Joseph built Victoria's first skyscraper, the Sayward Building, which still stands on Douglas Street at View.

Ann died in 1870. Some years later, W.P. moved to a mansion on the north side of Upper Fort Street, as it was then called. Farther up the hill stood "Erin Hall," the Nesbitts' fine home on the hill.

W.P. had worked hard all his life. By the time he retired in 1896, son Joseph had taken over the day-to-day running of the business. In later years Joseph developed the Sayward Farm at Elk Lake and built Victoria's first skyscraper, just down the street from where his mother and stepbrother were living when W.P. first entered their lives some 50 years before. It was constructed at a cost of $200,000—a fortune in those days—and completed in 1910.

By that time, W.P. was long gone. He had moved to San Francisco soon after he retired, and he died there in 1905. His body was returned to Victoria and buried, with full ceremony, at Ross Bay Cemetery. He is remembered in Sayward Street, Sayward Road, and the Sayward Building, which stands to this day on the northeast corner of Douglas and View, a monument to the pioneer lumberman who helped build this town.

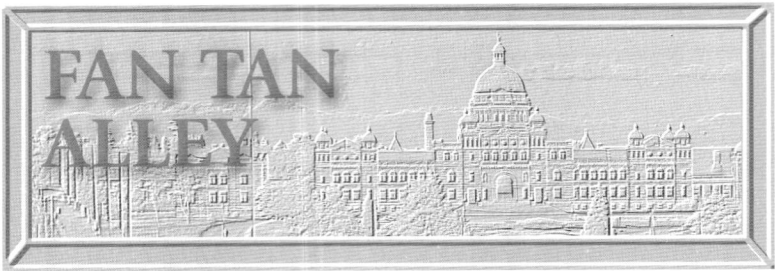

If those old walls could only talk

Some say it's the narrowest street in North America, but to the people who lived there toward the end of the nineteenth century, it was home.

Like so many others, the Chinese were drawn first to San Francisco, then to Victoria and the mainland by the promise of good fortune in the gold fields. As far as some of Victoria's merchants were concerned, Chinese gold-seekers were as welcome as any others looking for licences, supplies, clothing, food, and accommodation. Business was brisk for those who, in one way or another, catered to the hungry hordes.

A few of those Chinese visitors stayed in Victoria. Others travelled on to the Fraser River, returning to China when the gold ran out. For those who decided not to leave Victoria, "home" was a row of wooden shacks just north of the site of the HBC fort.

In the late 1850s a deep ravine ran west from the Cook Street marsh to the harbour, between today's Cormorant and Johnson streets. It was spanned by a wooden footbridge at Government Street. The western end of this ravine had served as the settlement's first burying ground from 1843 until 1855, when land was acquired on the outskirts of town (today's Quadra Street) for a cemetery that we now call Pioneer Square. The north side of the ravine is where Victoria's first Chinese sojourners made their homes.

No matter where they congregated, the Chinese always stayed close together in order to preserve and protect their identity and traditions. Their dense, close-knit communities were usually confined to one or two streets. Whites called these areas "Chinatown." They were characterized by wood-frame buildings where people lived practically on top of each other in what, to the whites, appeared to be perfect harmony. In fact, overcrowding spawned disease, crime, and poverty.

By 1861, Chinese people owned and populated the city block now bounded by Douglas, Fisgard, Store, and Pandora streets, as well as some lots a few blocks to the north and south and along the nearby waterfront. Most commercial activities—stores and other businesses—were centred on Cormorant. Today, Centennial Square and Lower Pandora give little hint of this once-thriving commercial centre.

As the years went by, a head tax of $500 was levied on all Chinese entering Canada. But while some people insisted that Chinese immigration should cease, others were happy to have it continue. Chinese people were hard workers,

Always ready with a smile, Chinese fish, fruit, and vegetable sellers brought fresh foods right to Victoria doorsteps.

Wee and Chew were the Chinese houseboys for Francis Rattenbury and his family in Oak Bay.

deferential, uncomplaining. Moreover, they were willing to perform menial tasks that white men refused—labouring, market gardening, laundering, and domestic work.

Many of the wealthy or reasonably well-to-do families arriving here in the early years had no idea how to run a household in a strange—or for that matter familiar—environment. Nor did they see any need to learn while there were people ready and willing to serve them.

Few of these homes were without a Chinese servant. As early as the 1860s, Sarah Crease, wife of Attorney-General Henry Crease, waxed eloquent about the virtues of their "charming Chinaman." Years later a young Emily Carr would assume that every family was fortunate enough to have a Bong or someone similar.

Chinese immigration reached its peak during the last decade of the nineteenth century and the first decade of the twentieth. More than 3,000 Chinese lived in the six-block area that was Chinatown. Brick buildings replaced many of the wood-frame structures; some of those that were left housed opium dens and factories, which were legal until 1908.

Almost all of Chinatown's inhabitants were male. Most of them laboured long and hard for little money. Far from their families, these men

Looking north from the townsite over the Johnson Street ravine circa 1890, wooden Chinese dwellings line Cormorant (now Pandora) Street.

found their own amusements in typical Chinese pursuits, including the theatre, celebration of traditional festivals, visits to the temple, and indoor games such as chess, chuck-luck, and Fan Tan.

Fan Tan is a Chinese game of chance—a board game with strict rules and high stakes. In Victoria's male-oriented Chinatown, gambling dens and brothels operated side by side. Fan Tan gambling clubs were known as Fan Tan Guan. By the early 1920s, most were concentrated in the heart of Chinatown, in a place that had become known as Fan Tan alley.

The alley was actually a passageway between adjoining lots that linked Pandora (as that part of Cormorant is now known) and Fisgard streets. The lots' uneven boundaries left it one metre wide at one end, two metres wide at the other. There were wooden doors at either end of the passageway. Entry was permitted only when authorized by a watchman. Inside the gambling dens, hidden doors opened onto escape routes out of windows and over rooftops that often foiled police. One raid in 1916, however, netted a catch of almost 100 players at the Oriental Club. The next day's *Daily Colonist* reported the location of the unfortunate gamblers' capture as "Fan Tan alley"—and so it has been known ever since.

Fan Tan Alley

After the end of the Second World War, when immigration laws affecting Chinese were relaxed, more Chinese families came to Canada, and gambling ceased to be a prime leisure time focus. A hundred years after the Chinese first settled in Victoria, only one Fan Tan club remained. Today, there are none.

Visitors to Fan Tan Alley these days will find nothing more decadent than restaurants, offices, and stores. Yet that narrow, brick-lined lane and the unique area that surrounds it provide a fascinating link with this city's colourful past.

This 1959 view along Fan Tan Alley, sometimes described as the narrowest street in North America, shows no hint of the intriguing activities of days gone by.

This monument at the Chinese Cemetery on Harling Point (once called Chinese Point) displays the Feast of the Dead. The cemetery, situated on a good Feng Shui—in harmony with Nature—site, was in use from 1903 till 1950. In recent years it has been restored, and a plaque recognizes the cultural contribution of the early Chinese community.

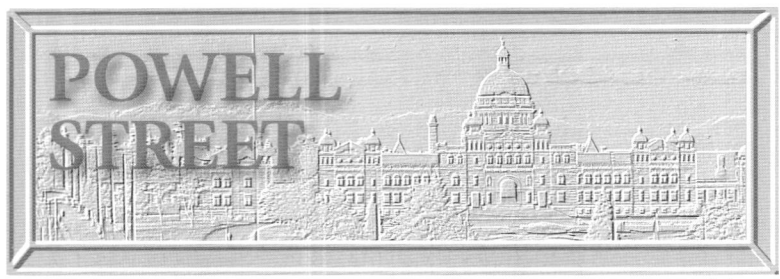

Victoria's first Canadian-born physician

Buried in the heart of James Bay is a small street with a long history, although the man it's named after lived some distance away.

Israel Wood Powell was descended from a long line of Welshmen who hailed from the town of Aberystwyth. There had been Powells in Canada, however, since the late 1780s. His ancestors were Empire Loyalists, and Powell himself was a true-blue Canadian, born in 1836 at Port Colborne, Upper Canada. He studied medicine at McGill University, qualifying at the age of 24. Two years later he left Montreal, bound for New Zealand. He got as far as Victoria—and decided to stay.

Powell liked the little city. He didn't feel out of place among the predominantly British residents and didn't mind being the only physician who had not graduated from an English university.

In later life, Dr. Israel Wood Powell looked every inch the prominent personage he had become.

The *Colonist* newspaper announced his arrival, saying that his excellent testimonials would stand him in good stead and that "Dr. I.W. Powell, MD, physician, surgeon and accoucheur" had his "rooms and residence at the Anglo-American Hotel, corner of Yates and Douglas."

He was one of the city's most eligible bachelors. Just under six feet tall, he had a long, bushy, black beard that flowed down over an immaculate collar and tie, almost reaching the top button of his vest. He was a fine horseman, interested in sports, and loved a good debate. Naturally, he was drawn to politics.

In 1863 he stood as a candidate for the House of Assembly of Vancouver Island. He was duly elected at a meeting chaired by Mayor Thomas Harris and threw himself into community affairs, volunteering his services to the fire department and the rifle corps, and championing the cause

Jennie and Israel Powell with an unnamed friend are pictured in Venice.

of education. In this last endeavour he was supported by medical colleague Dr. W.F. Tolmie, who joined him in lobbying for free schools. Eventually, Powell became the first chair of the Board of Education.

Somehow or other, he found time for romance. If he didn't get as far as New Zealand, he could do the next best thing—marry a New Zealander. Jennie Branks was born there in 1845 of Scottish parents. She had arrived in Victoria via San Francisco, where her family had relocated during the gold rush of 1849. In 1861 she visited a sister in Victoria. When she returned two years later, she met the handsome doctor. They were married at the Alexander Munro mansion, at the corner of Katherine (now Douglas) and Michigan Streets, in 1865.

Powell's interest in political affairs now assumed a national focus. He had always believed that Vancouver Island and the mainland should belong not to England or to the United States, but to Canada. He shared Prime Minister Sir John A. Macdonald's opinion that British Columbia should enter Confederation, and he spoke strongly and eloquently in its favour.

In 1871 he was in Ottawa with Joseph Trutch for the Senate debates. Trutch later returned to become B.C.'s first lieutenant-governor, but it was Powell who brought news of the final bill to Victoria, along with a Canadian flag that he presented to the volunteer fire department. No matter that it was the wrong flag—a Blue Ensign rather than the traditional Red Ensign. It was Canadian and was carried at the head of the celebratory procession with pride.

After Confederation, Powell accepted the

When British Columbia joined Confederation in 1871, Dr. Powell returned from Ottawa and presented a Canadian flag to the Deluge Fire Department, pictured here on Upper Yates Street in 1878.

position of Commissioner of Indian Affairs. He cared a great deal about the Native population. During the next seventeen years he travelled far and wide, helping to establish schools and improve medical care. His efforts did not go unnoticed. In recognition of his many journeys up the coast, the captain of the *Rocket* named a coastal settlement Powell River.

The *Colonist*, which a few years earlier, had chastised him roundly for irregular attendance at House of Assembly meetings, now trumpeted his success. "Truly," it declared, "few men have left such a splendid record of unselfish devotion and achievement for the public good." He retired as commissioner in 1889.

By the early 1880s, when it became clear that the promised transcontinental railway would finally reach as far as the coast, Powell lobbied for its terminus to be located in the town of Granville rather than Port Moody, and he donated land there for the first city hall. Granville—later renamed Vancouver—rewarded him by naming a downtown street in his honour.

Education remained a primary focus. In 1890 his efforts to establish a seat of higher learning were rewarded when the legislature passed an act creating the University of British Columbia. Powell was its first chancellor. He was also first president of the B.C. Medical Council. And by this time he was ready for a well-earned retirement.

During their early married life the Powells had lived at Fort and Douglas, where most of their nine children were born. In the early 1880s Powell had a fine home built for his family on a corner lot at Burdett Avenue and Vancouver Street. "Oakdene" was an imposing dwelling, with high ceilings, doors leading from the dining room out onto the lawn, wide bay windows overlooking the garden, and a conservatory.

Jennie was a firm favourite on the local scene and a force for cultural activities. She sang in St. Andrew's Presbyterian Church choir and was a member of St John's Church for more than four decades. She helped found several groups, including the Ladies' Musical Club and the Shakespeare Club, and was a member of the Alexandra Club, a forum for the study and appreciation of art, literature, and music.

The Powells celebrated their golden wedding anniversary at "Oakdene" in 1915. Sadly, Powell died shortly afterwards following a stroke. He was 77. Jennie moved in with one of her daughters. A widow for more than thirteen years,

"Oakdene," near the corner of Burdett Avenue and Vancouver Street, boasted beautiful gardens and a conservatory. Dr. Powell's hitching post stood outside the gate.

she died in 1928 at the age of 83 and was buried beside her husband at Ross Bay Cemetery. "Oakdene" was sold and became the episcopal residence of the Diocese of British Columbia, renamed "Bishop's Close."

The pioneering Powells were gone, but their name lives on in a West Coast town, a Vancouver street, and a short road just south of the Legislative Buildings in Victoria's James Bay.

TIEDEMANN PLACE

Architect to the colony

Just north of Powell's street are the Legislative Buildings, which in 1898 replaced the wooden structures designed 40 years earlier by Hermann Otto Tiedemann.

When Berlin-born Tiedmann (originally there was no second e in his name) arrived in Victoria in 1858, he was 37 years old. One of the most interesting periods of his life was about to begin. It was now fifteen years since the HBC had established a fort on the Inner Harbour. Stimulated some months earlier by the stampede of prospectors bound for the Fraser River, Victoria's economy was on the upswing. The area surrounding the fort was festooned with wooden shacks and shanties. Saloons and supply stores lined the dusty downtown streets.

Training as a civil engineer equipped Tiedemann for a position with the surveyor-general's department under J.D. Pemberton.

Hermann Otto and Mary Tiedemann

Within eighteen months he had distinguished himself by designing two quite different monuments: a handsome lighthouse and a not-so-handsome set of administrative buildings.

By mid-1858, Governor James Douglas realized that Fort Victoria was ill-equipped to handle the gold rush. Declaring that the fort was to be demolished, he sold the land surrounding it and used the proceeds to pay for a new colonial administration centre on the harbour's sloping southern shore. Tiedemann, he announced, was the architect of choice.

Perhaps inspired by the fact that wooden buildings often fell prey to the ravages of fire, Tiedemann decided to play it safe. He designed not one, but five buildings in a cluster. Together they comprised the strangest set of structures Victorians had ever seen.

Treading carefully across the wooden bridge that now spanned the muddy waters of James Bay, the town's citizens observed the new seat of

Tiedemann Place

Completed in 1859, Tiedemann's strange-looking Legislative Buildings caused much laughter amongst the locals, who called them the Birdcages. They were replaced in 1898 by the present-day buildings.

colonial government with a careful and critical eye. Some heaped praise on the architect. Others, like *Colonist* editor Amor De Cosmos, swamped him in a sea of scorn. The new administrative buildings, declared De Cosmos, left a lot to be desired. In fact, he wrote in a scathing editorial, they didn't look like government buildings at all; squat and square, with uptilted, Chinese-style roofs, they looked more like a cross between a pagoda and a birdcage.

Tiedemann's next project—a lighthouse at the mouth of Esquimalt Harbour—inspired more respect. Built on small, rocky Fisgard Island, its 47-foot tower was crowned by an 18-foot-high lantern. Seemingly glued to the tower's side, a solid red-brick residence became home to B.C.'s first lightkeeper, George Davies, and his family.

A year later, in 1861, Tiedemann married Mary Bissett, sister of HBC official James Bissett, who had sailed to Victoria with his family aboard the *Jenny Ford*. The Bissetts lived in James Bay at what is now 140 Government Street. The Tiedemanns lived a few blocks away, at Menzies and Superior.

The architect may still have been smarting from De Cosmos's comments about the "Birdcages" when he turned his attentions to surveying once again. Businessman Alfred Waddington sent him up north in 1862 to find a route for Waddington's pet project—a wagon road from Bute Inlet to the Cariboo. A grand

Tiedemann's Victoria Law Courts building in Bastion Square, which now houses the Maritime Museum of B.C., established his reputation as the most important architect in the colony in the late 1880s.

idea became a cruel experiment in survival for Tiedemann and his companions. Deserted by their guides at the mouth of the Homathko River, they almost starved in their search for a trail across the mountains.

Eventually the idea was abandoned. Tiedemann returned safely to Victoria and busied himself with surveys for a plan to bring Elk Lake water to Victoria, then sailed aboard the *Emily Harris* for Nanaimo to survey the location of a new coal mine. Back in Victoria he designed several structures, including the Finlayson Building on Wharf Street. But it was the edifice on Bastion Street that cemented his place in Victoria's history.

Completed in 1889, the Victoria Law Courts (now the Maritime Museum) arose on the former site of a police barracks and jailhouse. It was a magnificent brick-faced building that contained an ornate open-cage elevator, installed to provide easier access to the third-floor courtroom. Tiedemann was proud of his latest endeavour, but he didn't live long to enjoy it. Death came suddenly at his James Bay home in 1891. He was mourned by his wife and children.

Tiedemann Creek and Glacier at the head of Bute Inlet, and Tiedemann Place in Gordon Head are reminders of a man who helped build this city more than a century ago.

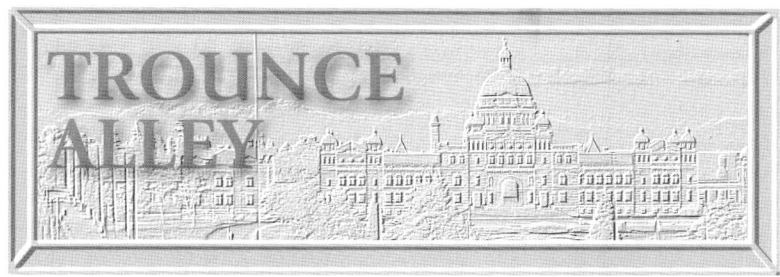

Alley builder trounced obstacles

Thomas Trounce arrived in Victoria the same year as H.O. Tiedemann—1858—but immediately established himself as an architect and builder in the fast-growing downtown core.

Trounce was born in Cornwall, England, in 1813. In the 1840s he and his wife Jane journeyed first to Van Dieman's Land, as Tasmania was called, then to California in search of gold. Both came from adventurous families. Shortly after they moved to Vancouver Island, they were joined by Jane's sister and brother-in-law, who had been living in Wisconsin.

The Trounces sailed to Victoria from San Francisco in 1858 in the same steamer as Thomas Fawcett, who would eventually have a store on Government Street near Trounce's property. Dropping anchor at Esquimalt after a crowded and uncomfortable eleven-day journey, they travelled by small steamer to Victoria Harbour and found a settlement still blinking its eyes in disbelief at the sight of hundreds upon hundreds of new arrivals.

The town wasn't prepared for the onslaught of Fraser River-bound miners. There were hardly any houses outside the HBC fort. On Fort Street itself, no more than a dirt trail in those days, fruit trees covered the land as far as Broad Street. East of what is now Douglas Street, Fort Street was lined with HBC barns, set back from the road. The muddy track that was Government Street had two-plank-deep, two-plank-wide sidewalks. Johnson Street was nothing but a deep ravine, crossed by wooden bridges at Store, Government, and Douglas streets. The only way to reach Beacon Hill Park or James Douglas's fine home across James Bay was via a long winding trail that followed the waterfront, although there were plans for a wooden bridge that would cut across the bay.

Thomas and Jane Trounce.

Eventually demolished in favour of a 44-unit apartment building, "Tregew" initially fronted on Superior Street. Later, the back of the house became the front, facing onto Michigan Street, opposite Captain John Irving's home (now Irving Park).

Like so many new arrivals in those early gold-rush days, the Trounces found the only place to stay was in one of the hundreds of tents that sprouted, like mushrooms, in the Douglas and Johnson area. They probably didn't mind. Canvas was preferable to any of the wooden shacks that had been hastily erected to accommodate gold miners passing through town. And soon they would move to more comfortable premises—a frame cottage on Kane (today's Broughton) Street.

It didn't take Trounce long to establish himself in business as an architect and builder. The more he looked at James Bay, the more he liked the thought of a permanent home there. In 1861 he bought an acreage near the "Birdcages," and he built himself a fine home— the first stone dwelling, some say, in Victoria.

Trounce's property, not far from Tiedemann's, was contained on three sides by Menzies, Superior, and Michigan streets. A little farther over, toward Beacon Hill Park and closer to the ocean, wholesale merchant Richard Carr was looking at a similar piece of land for his own home. Trounce's was finished first, and he called it "Tregew."

Trounce built his home so that it fronted onto Superior Street, facing the harbour, like

Trounce Alley

In the 1880s, John Kurtz's cigar factory stood near the corner of Trounce Alley and Government Street.

the governor's mansion. Later, when the land was subdivided, access to the house was from Michigan, across from the home of Captain John Irving of the Canadian Pacific Navigation Company. "Tregew" was Number 436. Its two-foot-thick, uncoursed fieldstone walls, supported at the corners by dressed stone blocks, set it apart from the wooden structures of the day. The shallow roof was decorated with elaborate eaves. French doors opened from the dining room onto a pillared verandah, which looked out over beautiful gardens. In his greenhouse—one of the first in Victoria—Trounce grew exotic plants and sold them at auctions. He won awards for a display of apples grown in his own orchard at the southwest corner of Superior and Menzies streets.

Meanwhile, he concentrated on building up his business. One of his first major projects was the police barracks, used as a jail until 1889 when it was replaced by Tiedemann's Law Courts on Bastion Street.

In the mid-1860s Trounce was responsible for building and managing naval storehouses and wharves at Esquimalt Harbour. Esquimalt was then a major port, servicing large steamers from San Francisco that each carried between 1,000 and 1,500 passengers and 1,000 tons of freight.

He bought prime land on the block between Government and Broad streets and leased it to storeowners. Then came a nasty surprise. He had been told that View Street was to be extended right through to Wharf Street. It made sense—after all, what was a View Street without a view?

More than two decades before Robert Dunsmuir's Craigdarroch Castle loomed atop the Fort Street hill, "Armadale," designed by Trounce for Senator William J. Macdonald, lorded it over the southwest corner of James Bay.

But the land at Broad Street was sold to a Mr. Southgate, who promptly fenced it, and View Street came to an abrupt halt. Now the unfortunate shopper had to dogleg along Broad Street to Yates or Fort and walk down to Government Street in order to reach Trounce's tenants' stores.

Trounce solved the problem by building a lane through his property so that his tenants' customers could have access. Trounce Avenue was born. All Trounce had to do to retain title to the land was to close the alley for one day of each year to prove that it was indeed private property.

By 1876, Trounce was a member of Victoria city council and a successful architect responsible for several commercial downtown structures—including the Green Building on Broad Street and John Weiler's furniture factory (now the Counting House) on Broughton at Broad—as well as magnificent homes like Senator William J. Macdonald's "Armadale" in James Bay. He was also an upstanding pillar of the community and a solid supporter of the Methodist Church.

Services had been held in a police court room on Bastion Street until 1859, when the first Methodist Church was built "just outside the city" on the corner of Broad and Pandora. Parishioners gained entrance to the church by crossing a water-filled gully on a stilted sidewalk. In the church basement there were Sunday School classes, prayer meetings, and lectures. Tea meetings were presided over by Mrs. Trounce

Trounce was a solid supporter of Victoria's first Methodist Church, built on the southwest corner of Broad and Pandora streets in 1859. Mrs. Trounce presided over the post-Sunday service tea-pouring.

and her friend Emma Spencer, whose husband, David, owned the magnificent department store just south of Trounce's alley. Trounce became Grand Master of the Masonic Temple in 1885.

Three years later Jane died, at the age of 72. In 1889, Trounce married Emma Richards in San Francisco. They honeymooned in Australia before settling in James Bay. Trounce died there eleven years later, in June 1900, aged 87. Emma was laid to rest beside him at Ross Bay Cemetery in 1902.

"Tregew" is gone, but Trounce Alley remains as a quaint reminder of the man who didn't let a T-junction take the edge off his business success.

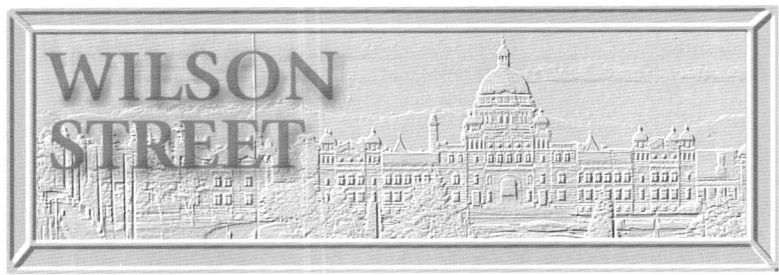

Clothing capped brothers' success

No one was happier about Thomas Trounce's decision to build an alleyway than William Wilson. His business might have been just another one in a row, but thanks to Trounce's alley, Wilson's clothing store ended up on a corner, with double the display window space to entice passersby.

Born in London, England, in 1838, Wilson seemed set for a lifetime of secure living as an accountant in the silk manufacturing company where his father was a working partner, but then the unthinkable happened. French tariffs on silks led to the collapse of the business. Fortunately, other prospects loomed. The *London Times* talked constantly of gold in the Cariboo. Wilson, now 24, decided to sail around Cape Horn to find it.

When his ship anchored at Esquimalt in 1862, Wilson found the city of Victoria, newly incorporated, brimming with business opportunities. The Cariboo was a lot farther away than he had thought, and it would cost a great deal to transport the dry goods and clothing he had brought with him. Why not sell them in Victoria and invest the proceeds in a local venture?

He bought the stock of a firm that had gone bankrupt and opened his own store on the premises. It was just a simple log building on the east side of Government Street, but business was brisk —so brisk that the next spring he decided to follow his original plan and check out the Cariboo. The Victoria store was left in the capable hands of brother Joseph, newly arrived from England via Panama and the West Coast aboard the same steamer that brought David Spencer, soon to be a business neighbour.

William summered in Barkerville, wintered in Victoria. Four years later, with the Cariboo

William Wilson was the first of three generations to run a downtown clothing store. He is shown here with his wife Elizabeth.

Wilson Street

Looking north along a plank-sidewalked Government Street from Fort Street in the 1860s, the low building in the right foreground is the Brown Jug Saloon on the southeast corner. Next to it is the forerunner of the Eaton Centre. Farther along the street, indicated by the arrow, W. & J. Wilson's store stands as it does today on the northeast corner of Government and Trounce Alley.

W. & J. Wilson men's clothing store a success and the mines worked out, William returned to Victoria for good. Joseph had not been idle. Their father, Joseph Wilson Sr., still in England, assured a steady supply of merchandise. Profits continued to climb.

So busy was he with his busy-ness, you'd think William would have no time for romance. But one day in 1864 he met a young woman who was visiting her sister and brother-in-law in Victoria. Elizabeth Eilbeck had travelled from Cumberland, England, via Salt Lake City and San Francisco to visit Isabella Turner. William, a friend of the Turners, was invited to dinner. He and Elizabeth fell in love. They were married on New Year's Day, 1865. Their union would last 40 years and produce six children.

Meanwhile, W. & J. Wilson's became a much-respected business in Victoria. It was little wonder the brothers did so well. Government Street was still the heart of downtown. In the days before door-to-door delivery, their location, right opposite the old post office, guaranteed steady traffic with every bi-weekly mail boat. A reputation for quality fabrics and finely tailored garments from the Old Country attracted a faithful following and guaranteed growth. In the 1870s, the log building on Government Street was demolished in favour of more modern premises in which to house their store, and eventually W. & J. Wilson's spread its wings to several other cities in Western Canada.

William's business interests also included coal mining. Two of his sons, groomed for business success, opened a wholesale grocery on Wharf Street. He maintained a high profile in the community by serving for many years as a member of the school board and, from 1878 to 1882, as a member of the provincial legislature.

William Wilson moved out of his St. Charles Street home and into the Hotel Dallas, on the James Bay waterfront north of Ogden Point, after his wife died and his children married and left home. The 60-room, "strictly first class" hotel, with its rooftop promenade deck and panoramic views, declined in popularity when the new steamship terminal lured passengers to the Inner Harbour. The hotel, which stood north of Ogden Point, was demolished in 1928.

Joseph, who never married and never sought the public eye, died in 1900. His nephew, also called Joseph, William's eldest son, who had joined the business some sixteen years earlier, managed the store. It prospered through the years of growth, when mining, lumber, sealing, whaling, fishing, and the Canadian Pacific Railroad fuelled British Columbia's expansion.

In 1905, and again in 1912, the company's premises were enlarged to supply the demand for quality clothing. The little store on Government Street became a prominent establishment on a corner of the alley that funnelled Broad Street browsers right through to the Wilsons' front door.

The William Wilson home on St. Charles Street was a very social place—five sons and a daughter saw to that. Life was not without sadness, however. Elizabeth died at the age of 60, two years before Joseph.

As each son and daughter married in turn, the St. Charles Street home seemed more and more like an empty shell. William moved into the Hotel Dallas on the waterfront near Ogden Point, not far from his daughter Millie. In 1922, William died at his daughter's home at the age of 84 and was buried beside Elizabeth at Ross Bay Cemetery.

There were many enterprising Wilsons in Victoria in those early years. There's a Wilson Street in Vic West. Wilson Street in Oak Bay, which did relate to the Wilsons of our story, has long since been renamed. But here's a toast to them all, and an extra-hearty cheer for the brothers whose store survives in Victoria to this day.

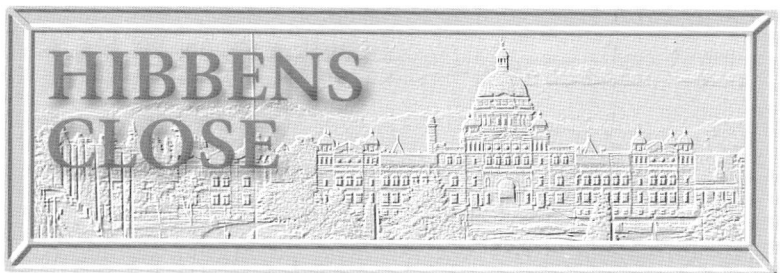

Early bookstore set stage for debate

On the opposite side of Government Street to the Wilsons' clothing store and Trounce's alley stood Thomas Hibben's bookstore.

Thomas Napier Hibben was born and educated in Charleston, South Carolina. At 21, ripe for adventure, he travelled to San Francisco in search of riches. He made money at the mines and invested it in a bookstore and stationery business that did well for him and equipped him for a move farther north ten years later, when gold fever struck again. Mid-1858 found him sailing into Esquimalt along with all the other fortune-hunters.

There were already two bookstores in the settlement. Hibben bought one of them—Kierski's on the south side of Yates Street—and thus began a tradition that would survive well into the next century.

Books were much in demand in those early days when colonists far from home thirsted for news and reading materials, and, just as in San Francisco, Hibben found a ready market for his business. With partner James Carswell, he set up a combined printing and bookselling business that became one of the most successful in town. Just inside the settlement's boundaries, Yates Street bustled with publishing activity of every sort. Two newspapers—the *Victoria Gazette* and the *British Colonist*—chronicled the growth of the former HBC post. Not far from Hibben's store, Alfred Waddington was hard at work on his book, *The Fraser Mines Vindicated*, which was the colony's first non-government publication.

T.N. Hibben

In 1862, Victoria officially became a city, with a mayor, more than 400 eligible voters, and a vibrant future. Its streets spread out like fingers, ever farther from their beginnings around the old fort. The eastern boundary crept over to Douglas Street. Buildings now had numbers. Hibben's bookstore on Yates Street was Number 37.

By this time he was firmly established in his new surroundings. Bookstores and reading rooms were favoured places for the men of the town to gather for animated discussions about business and politics. Hibben's premises provided a platform for this activity, a nucleus of ideas and opinions that could be shared with

In the 1880s, T.N. Hibben's stationery store was a popular fixture on Government Street, particularly with Victoria's children. In her writings, Emily Carr recalled how at Christmastime, Hibben would put the school books at the back of the shelves, leaving the more interesting and enticing story books open at the front.

others at James Fell's grocery, Thomas Shotbolt's pharmacy, and Mayor Thomas Harris's meat market, all within easy walking distance of his Yates Street store.

There was much to discuss. HBC influence had diminished, and there was talk of uniting Vancouver's Island with the mainland. The fort was being dismantled. As the last of its buildings bit the dust in 1864, Hibben took a wife. He and Janet Parker Brown were married in January and produced the first of their two sons later that same year.

Not long afterwards, James Carswell left to set up a legal publishing firm that was the first of its type and thrives to this day. Hibben continued the business on his own as T.N. Hibben & Co. His store was a firm favourite with local children. Years later, Edgar Fawcett recalled how as a schoolboy he visited the store, and Emily Carr wrote in her *Book of Small* about the "Merry Christmas" sign in Hibben's window, and how he delighted her by "hiding all the school books behind story books left open at the best pictures."

Three decades after its opening, Hibben's store enjoyed continued growth. Advertised as "Importing Stationers and Booksellers," it declared itself "prepared to furnish nearly every variety of stationery in use," printing, ruling and binding, Admiralty coast charts, photographic albums, mathematical instruments, fine pocket cutlery, wrapping paper, music, and much, much more.

Eventually, the store was relocated round the corner on Government Street, on land owned by J.J. Southgate. It was Southgate who erected a fence at Broadway (now Broad Street) to enclose his newly purchased property and promptly erected commercial buildings behind it, on land that had once been a vegetable patch. This simple-sounding move wrought complex results, for it brought a westbound street that displayed every intention of running parallel with Fort and Yates streets to the harbour to an abrupt halt. By the time the fence was removed, other buildings had filled the gap where a road was supposed to run. Thus we have Bastion Street, a short, narrow thoroughfare that some say was originally intended as the continuation of present-day View Street.

Hibben's original Government Street building burned down during the fire that demolished the nearby Spencer arcade. From its ashes arose an even more impressive building, its five floors topped by a neon sign depicting St. George and the dragon. Hibben would have been proud of it, but by this time he was gone, dead at 62 and buried at Ross Bay Cemetery. His two sons carried on the business for their mother, along with two key employees, C.W. Kammerer and W.H. Bone.

The Hibben-Bone Building, built in 1910 by Hibben's sons, was once famous for the enormous rooftop pencil that advertised its wares. Today the building, little changed, houses the Bedford Regency Hotel.

Today, Hibbens Close at Cadboro Bay reminds us of that long-ago pioneering family. A short cul-de-sac, it leads to the top of a cliff overlooking the water, affording a view as expansive as the one held by a bookstore owner who made Victoria his home all those years ago.

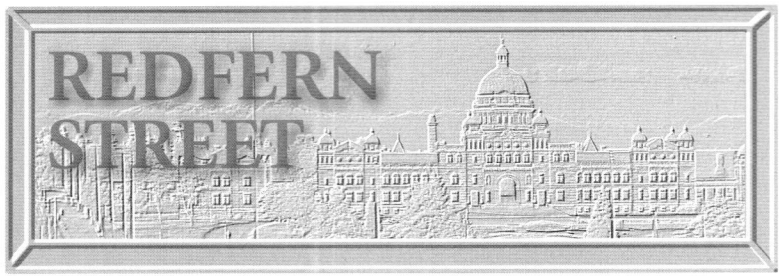

Clockmaker wound up as mayor

Within two short blocks on Government Street, John Weiler, William Wilson, and Thomas Hibben all found innovative ways to advertise their wares. But nothing captivated customers like Redfern's clock.

Charles Redfern was a Londoner by birth and a clockmaker by trade, who had apprenticed with his father before striking out on his own. Considering it was so specialized, clockmaking paid poorly. By the spring of 1862, Redfern was geared for greener pastures, ready to leave his homeland for the promise of gold in the Cariboo.

As he boarded the vessel *Tynemouth*, Redfern was probably aware that his travelling companions included more women than one might expect. He was in fair company indeed. This was the famous "bride ship," its complement of 62 women destined to become wives of gold miners and others who had gravitated here.

The *Tynemouth*'s summer voyage was shorter than most but not without mishap. The crew threatened mutiny, coal-stokers went on strike, and storm waves broke over the bow. Redfern, a small, dapper man with a neatly trimmed beard and bright eyes, took it all in his stride, leading his fellow passengers in the same way he would later lead fellow citizens in his adopted home.

Charles Redfern

The *Tynemouth* anchored safely at Esquimalt in mid-September. Somewhere on the long walk into town, Redfern changed his mind about gold mining. Here was an exciting new city, a population that included people with fine homes and carriages—and not a clockmaker in sight.

A year later, after finding work where he could and saving every cent, Redfern was able to start up a jewellery and clockmaking business. Soon he was able to send for his mother, now widowed, and his two sisters and install them in a comfortable home in James Bay. By 1875 he had bought out another jeweller and established himself on Government Street. Two years later he was ready to take a bride.

Eliza Arden Robinson, also British-born, was twelve years his junior. The two were married

Pictured at their James Bay home overlooking the Inner Harbour, Charles and Liza Redfern (centre) are surrounded by their children. At back, from left: Will, Martha Eliza (known as Pattie), Ina, Harry. Front, from left: Kate, Alfred, Winnifred, Elsie, and Alice.

in 1877 at St. John's Church on Douglas Street, where the Bay stands today, and lived near the corner of St. John (now Pendray) and Belleville streets. Their home was soon filled with fun and laughter, as one Redfern baby followed another. Over the next fourteen years, a total of three sons and six daughters joined the family.

It was a wonderful place to grow up. The children played safely on an open, grassy lot owned by their father across Belleville Street (long since swallowed up by the Laurel Point development), enjoying a panoramic view from the Sooke Hills in the west, across the harbour to the mouth of the Gorge waterway, and around to the wooden bridge spanning James Bay.

In 1877, Redfern, a reputable businessman and fine family man, eager to contribute to his community, became an alderman for James Bay ward. As a debater, accomplished amateur actor, and confident chorister, he was adept at expressing himself in public and parlayed that ability into a political career that spanned two decades.

By now, everyone knew Redfern's store. Not only did he regularly take out newspaper advertisements extolling the virtue of items

In 1891, Redfern obtained and installed the clocks that still show the time atop Victoria City Hall.

personally selected by him in Europe and the United States. He also had a gimmick that was guaranteed to get attention every minute of the day—a magnificent clock that hung above the sidewalk outside his store.

Ordered especially from England, it was Victoria's first town clock and remained a wonder for many decades to come. No matter which direction one walked along Government Street, its huge face could be seen clearly. And to the chagrin of those living or working close by, its bell could be heard equally clearly. In 1884, when Redfern moved into new premises at 43 Government Street, the clock went too. Some said its hourly chimes carried clear out to Oak Bay.

The year before his move, Redfern had become the city's fifteenth mayor, determined to help create good roads, a more adequate water supply, and better sewerage. Over the next sixteen years of defeat and re-election, he served the city well.

In 1891, Redfern installed Victoria's most famous clock—the one atop City Hall, bringing it in under budget at $5,000. He was also responsible, during his final year as mayor, for

Redfern Street

The Charles E. Redfern, *pictured on Government Street during its annual testing in the early 1900s, has been restored to its former glory.*

raising $4,950 toward the purchase of a new, state-of-the-art steam pumper for fighting fires.

When it arrived from Brantford, Ontario, it was named in his honour. And what a sight it was! Handsomely finished with Russian iron lagging, heavy brass spun bands, and a nickel dome, the *Charles E. Redfern* could achieve 100 p.s.i. in just over ten minutes and throw a single stream of water 210 feet. Two horses hurtled it along wood-blocked downtown streets. A century later, lovingly restored, it worked as well as the day it arrived.

Redfern's last mayoral term saw construction of permanent sidewalks, a new Legislative Building at one end of the James Bay causeway, and a new post office at the other. They were sterling achievements. But in the first two decades of the new century, his fortunes changed. His mother, a sister, and his beloved wife died. In 1914, in the depression preceding the First World War, Redfern's business went bankrupt. He worked for the Marine Department for five years until his retirement in 1922 and remained active until he died of a stroke in 1929, in his 89th year. He was buried, with his family, at Ross Bay.

Redfern Street, just west of Foul Bay Road, and Redfern Park at its northern end bear witness to the passing of this remarkable man. The fire engine named in his honour has been preserved for posterity. The building that housed his jewellery store stands to this day at 1019 Government Street. The only thing missing is Redfern's magnificent clock, which still keeps good time in the tower of a church at Cowichan.

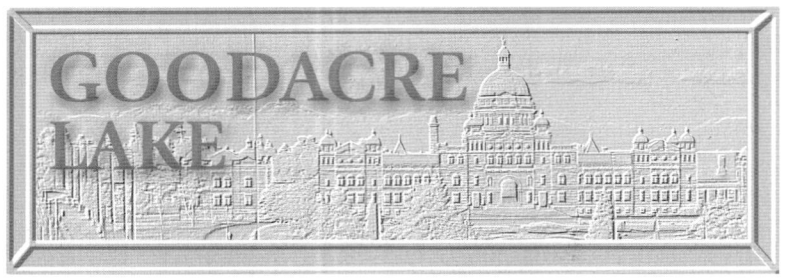

In the market for meat and vegetables

Well within chiming distance of Redfern's jewellery store, Lawrence Goodacre's meat market was doing a roaring trade.

Goodacre was born in Nottinghamshire, England, in 1848, the son of a corn factor and miller. He had other ideas for his own career, however. At the age of sixteen, when he left school, he apprenticed as a butcher until he was ready to strike out on his own. In 1865 he left England, travelled via San Francisco, and sailed into Esquimalt the following spring. The adventurous new arrival was just eighteen years old.

Lawrence and Maria Goodacre

He came ashore to find a growing city on the eve of glory. Victoria was about to become the official capital of the colony of British Columbia, and there was talk of Confederation. It was a splendid spot for an ambitious young fellow with a solid background in butchering. Life might be unpredictable, but one thing you could count on: people would always have to eat.

A few short years later, Goodacre went into partnership with one John Stafford, who had recently taken over a business on the southeast corner of Government and Johnson streets. The two were following in famous footsteps; the first proprietor of the Queen's Market had been Thomas Harris, first butcher in business and Victoria's first mayor.

Stafford & Goodacre did well until Stafford became ill in 1876. Frail for some time, he sailed to Southern California in an effort to boost his health. But the lung problems that had plagued him didn't subside, and the following February he died. It was a shock to Victorians. Stafford had been here since 1862, and worst of all, he was only 40 years old when he died.

Goodacre was left to pick up the pieces.

A venerable Lawrence Goodacre, pictured front row, second from right, sits for the formal Victoria city council portrait in 1904.

Having run the store by himself for some time, he felt confident that he could continue. When Stafford's grieving widow and children returned to Victoria, Goodacre looked after them also. The two men had been close friends as well as partners, so people were pleased and not overly surprised when, later in 1877, Maria Stafford became Goodacre's bride.

His ready-made family required a larger home, so he had a villa built for them on the north side of Pandora Street, just east of Blanshard. Everything was within easy walking distance—his store, the Methodist church on Broad Street, and the grand new City Hall, where Goodacre's penchant for politics would soon become apparent.

Queen's Market was quite the success story. Twenty-five years after he had opened its doors, Goodacre's wholesale and retail trade was a top money-producer in its class. His many contracts included Her Majesty's Royal Navy, the dominion government, and several large corporations, not to mention hotels, restaurants, and local households.

The Goodacre boys joined him in the business, which still occupied its prominent place at Government and Johnson streets. Slaughterhouses in the Mt. Tolmie area were kept busy supplying the market with meat. According to the *Colonist*, it took a daily total

Goodacre (standing far right) posed with his staff outside his Queen's Market at Government and Johnson streets.

Two of Goodacre's sons are pictured with some of the market staff. Left to right, back row: R. McFadden, George Tyson, Pete Fields; front row: Roy Goodacre, G. Mitchell, Sam Goodacre, Al Stevens.

Goodacre Lake

In Beacon Hill Park, the stone bridge across the lake that bears Lawrence Goodacre's name provided the perfect vantage point for feeding the swans that waited patiently there.

of 6 to 8 cattle, 35 sheep, and 10 calves and hogs to satisfy the demand for good quality product and keep the market supplied with meat. Goodacre employed eighteen people in different departments. He believed in customer service, often delivering the meat himself sooner than entrust it to clattering delivery carts.

While her husband's firm flourished, Maria Goodacre was far from idle. With children fathered by Lawrence added to her own, family life kept her busy, but she still found time to sing in the Methodist church choir conducted by David Spencer, and to help those less fortunate than herself.

She was particularly concerned about the plight of the elderly and was instrumental in founding the Home for Aged and Infirm Women. The homeless didn't escape her watchful eye. She and two others formed a committee that successfully persuaded Mayor Redfern to provide money toward a shelter for women with no place to stay.

Goodacre, meanwhile, had become more and more interested in politics. He was elected alderman for Johnson Street ward in 1889 and served on and off through 1906. By that time, an impressive new Legislative Building had long since replaced the "Birdcages." Access to the legislature was via a causeway that extended downtown Government Street to incorporate

In the early days, the path around Goodacre Lake afforded strollers a view of the fine homes that still stood along the west side of Douglas Street at that time.

the former Birdcage Walk. James Bay waves lapped at one side of the causeway; on the other, a stately new hotel was taking shape on reclaimed land.

After his wife died in 1918, at the age of 73, Goodacre continued to work at his store and involve himself in civic and social affairs. Only when he was 80 years old would he consider retirement. Seems it didn't suit him. Two years later he too was gone, a victim of heart disease at the age of 82, buried beside his wife at Ross Bay.

Today the Richard Blanshard Building stands on the site of Goodacre's home. However, there is no street to record his existence. If city fathers hadn't seen fit to rename Beacon Hill Park's largest lake in honour of his involvement with the Parks Board, we probably wouldn't remember him at all.

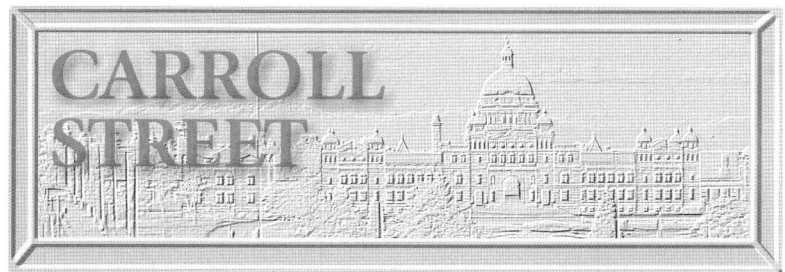

CARROLL STREET

He served ale in brown jugs

Just down Government Street from where Lawrence Goodacre established his butcher's shop, there is a small brick building that was once owned by John D. Carroll, landlord of Victoria's most colourful watering hole—the Brown Jug Saloon. Considering he lived in the area for only a few short years, Carroll managed to make quite a mark on impressionable Victorians of the day. He certainly did his best to keep them well watered.

Carroll was an Irishman who wandered far from home at an early age, following his money-making instincts as far as America and staying long enough to take out citizenship there. In 1858, after several years in California, he sailed for Vancouver Island, lured like all the others by the promise of Fraser River riches. In fact, Carroll never did mine for gold; he had others mine it for him, while he busied himself serving the residents of Victoria.

Carroll landed here when gold rush fever was high. He wasted no time setting up as a liquor merchant and grocer, with a store in the midst of all the action on Yates Street, between Government and Wharf. Prospectors flooded the place. Each ship that anchored brought more and more bodies. The tent town just north of Carroll's establishment expanded to accommodate temporary residents who were gathering gear and supplies for the gold fields. And everyone agreed there was nothing like gear-gathering for getting up a thirst.

It wasn't long before Carroll saw an opportunity to supplement his walk-in customer service with a sit-down location in the form of a downtown saloon. The Brown Jug was a hit from the moment it opened its doors, despite stiff competition from others close by. Living in Victoria in those early days seemed to bring out the imbibing instinct, as evidenced by the plethora of places serving plonk.

More than twenty hotels and saloons vied with each other for custom. The east side of Government Street, between Johnson and Humboldt, boasted no fewer than nine such establishments, each with its own lure for the liquor-loving man.

John D. Carroll, Irish entrepreneur and pioneer saloon-keeper.

Once a salubrious drinking place with an elegant glass-and-brass interior (pictured in 1902), the Brown Jug site on the southeast corner of Government and Fort streets is now occupied by a retail store.

But only one—Carroll's—served beer in brown bottles with a "Brown Jug" label.

Carroll's saloon was the fourth stop on the right for weary pedestrians walking north from the wooden bridge that spanned James Bay. It was on a street that was undergoing major changes by 1864, when the last buildings of the HBC fort disappeared. In their place, fine brick buildings jostled with the fire-prone wooden structures that had been erected so hastily in the face of the human onslaught some six years earlier. Victoria was now a city, with a mayor and a council, more than half a dozen churches, and a choice of three newspapers—included in the reading materials available at the Brown Jug Saloon—for those yearning for updates on local and worldly affairs.

Victoria's population was still swelling. Some gold miners, unlucky at the Fraser or the Cariboo, visited briefly on their journey home. Others, flush with success and gold burning holes in their pockets, settled here and formed a nucleus whose descendants would live to tell their tale.

Carroll was a keen volunteer with the Tiger Engine Company, pictured on Johnson Street in the 1870s.

Perhaps his own success went some way toward compensating Carroll for the losses in his life. His wife Adele, who had come with him from San Francisco, died in the fall of 1858 soon after their arrival. Carroll married again, this time to a woman named Ellen. They lived in a large brick home on the north side of Courtney Street, near Blanshard. Ellen had three children in three years. All of them died within hours of their birth. First was George Washington, born on the same day as the U.S. president. Next was John Thomas, who survived only for a few minutes. A year later, newborn Mary Margaret joined her brothers in the family grave.

Fortunately for Carroll, the store and saloon kept his mind off his sorrows. He had retained strong ties in San Francisco and travelled frequently between the two cities. One of his pet commercial projects was a passenger and freight wagon service between Esquimalt and Victoria, following the winding, muddy, three-mile forested trail that later became Old Esquimalt Road. A keen volunteer with the fire department in the Tiger Engine Company, he also became active in political circles and was an assessor for Lake, Esquimalt, and Metchosin districts. He set "a very excellent example," declared the *Colonist*, by donating his four-pound, eighteen-shilling salary to the Royal Hospital.

In four short years, Carroll had made a name for himself in Victoria. But like his infant children, he was not long for this world. In the spring of 1862 he fell ill. Diagnosed with consumption, he sailed to San Francisco in the hopes of finding a cure. By mid-July he was dead. His remains were brought back to Victoria and interred in the Old Burying Ground, next to his first wife and his children.

The Carroll monument, one of the few remaining in its original position in Pioneer Square, is a fitting reminder of a fellow whose short time amongst us was marked by sorrow and success. Another reminder, Carroll Street, runs north from Gorge Road, east of Tillicum, to Burnside Road.

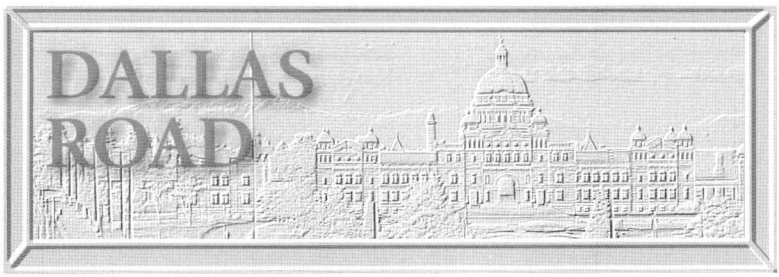

Married the governor's daughter

At some time or other, all of us have walked or driven along scenic Dallas Road with its breathtaking views of the Olympic Mountains. We won't forget its name. But we'd be forgiven for forgetting the man it's named after, because Alexander Grant Dallas didn't spend much time on these shores.

Dallas was born in British Guiana in 1816. His Scottish parents took their family back to Scotland, and Dallas was educated there. A successful business career in England and China positioned him favourably for election, in 1856, as a director of the HBC. Before long he was on a ship bound for Panama and Fort Vancouver, on the Columbia River. From there he travelled on to Fort Victoria, the HBC's western headquarters on the southern tip of Vancouver Island.

It was 1857. James Douglas was doing double duty as chief factor at the fort and governor of Vancouver Island. Despite his assurances to the contrary, HBC officials in London suspected he was becoming too caught up in governing the colony to pay proper attention to the company's affairs. Dallas was sent to help.

The two men were intelligent, strong, and opinionated, but there the similarity ended. Douglas was the product of a career in the field, with experience gained over almost four decades at several different, and often remote, fur trading posts. Dallas, on the other hand, was a businessman. He had never "roughed it," being used to a more civilized life in a world populated by bankers, financiers, and other influential people. Dr. J.S. Helmcken later described him as

Jane Douglas Dallas (left), and A.G. Dallas with his youngest son, Rupert.

Watching waves from Dallas Road during a heavy southeaster on October 17, 1920.

"shrewd, sharp, sensible ... fond of dogs and horses."

One of the shrewdest moves he made, one year after his arrival, was to marry into Victoria's first family. Like Helmcken before him, he was captivated by the Douglas girls. All five of them were shy and pretty. The oldest, Cecilia, was Helmcken's wife. Jane was five years Cecilia's junior and 23 years younger than the man who sought her hand. True love knows no birthdays. In March 1858, Dallas married the governor's daughter.

Little more than a month later, the *Commodore* sailed into Victoria Harbour, bringing the first of a wave of 20,000 prospectors bound for the newly discovered gold fields on the Fraser River. Shipload after shipload of men, most with experience of the gold rush in California, picked up licences and supplies and travelled on to Yale.

Spooked by the spectre of permanent American settlement on the mainland, the British government established a new colony named British Columbia. Douglas was forced to choose between his job as chief factor and the chance to be governor of both colonies. After more than 37 years with the HBC, he transferred his allegiance to the Crown. His son-in-law, Alexander Grant Dallas, took over as head of the HBC's Western Department.

Dallas Road

Dallas's road ran along the waterfront past Beacon Hill Park, becoming one with the racecourse (now Circle Drive) that once circled the base of Beacon Hill. This 1900 photo looks northwest across Goodacre Lake to Douglas Street.

Almost immediately he was involved in a war over a wandering pig on San Juan Island. Once a favourite picnic spot for Victorians, the island become the subject of dispute when an American squatter by the name of Lyman Cutler killed an HBC pig that had ventured onto his vegetable patch.

Dallas set sail on the *Beaver* to investigate and reported that he had, in essence, rapped Cutler's knuckles and warned him to stay out of trouble. The Americans had another slant on the story, saying that Dallas had ordered Cutler to pay a hefty fine or face a trial in Victoria. They didn't care for the notion of a British man threatening an American on what they perceived to be American soil. This dispute dragged on for a dozen years, until Kaiser Wilhelm of Germany ruled in 1872 that the San Juans were the sole property of the United States.

Dallas, meanwhile, was making his presence felt at home. He took his appointment to "The London Committee for Watching the Affairs of B.C." seriously. Douglas, he said, had no business declaring that Beacon Hill was a public park; Beacon Hill belonged to the HBC and Douglas had no right to give it away. Observing that the fur trade was fading fast, Dallas suggested to the HBC in London that the company's future lay in commercial ventures, thus laying the foundation for the chain of department stores that links Canadian cities to this day.

Life on the home front was less fractious. The Dallases' union was a happy one and produced nine children. As though to show he meant no ill by his remarks about Beacon Hill, Dallas named one of the boys James Douglas after his grandfather. The family lived on Government Street near Broughton, just beyond the fort property, a short distance from Jane's childhood home.

Although they never lived on it, Dallas Road was destined to become an important feature on the James Bay peninsula. In the early days it curved past shipyards and R.P. Rithet's wharves and ended at the Beacon Hill Park racetrack. Later, it was extended to Lover's Lane (today's Memorial Crescent). By 1891, a huge hotel stood near Rithet's wharves, north of today's Ogden Point.

The Hotel Dallas boasted 60 rooms, 12 sitting rooms and parlours, and accommodation for 100 guests. An observation tower afforded a clear view across to the Olympic Mountains, out beyond Race Rocks, and over toward the Sooke Hills. Steamers from China, Japan, Alaska, and San Francisco tied up at the docks across the street. Electric cars transported passengers from the hotel to the downtown area in just eight minutes. Modern appliances and conveniences included hot- and cold-water baths, steam heat, electric lights, bar and billiard rooms, and a rooftop promenade deck. The hotel, said its advertisers, "is strictly first class."

Rumour had it that a bridge was to be built across the harbour entrance, linking the railway yard on the former Songhees Indian Reservation with the docks at Ogden Point. The hotel was perfectly positioned to make a handsome profit. Unfortunately, the bridge didn't materialize. In 1908, the Empress Hotel lured visitors to the Inner Harbour, and a new steamship terminal in the harbour made it possible for vessels to tie up almost opposite. The Hotel Dallas's heyday was over, and it was demolished in 1928.

By that time, the Dallases were long gone. Dallas had been appointed governor of the HBC's northwest territories, known as Rupert's Land, in 1862 and had moved his family to Fort Garry (now Winnipeg). He and his father-in-law governed most of Canada. In 1864, Dallas retired to England and died there in 1882. Jane died in 1909.

Today's Dallas Road starts at the north end of Erie Street and ends on the eastern curve of Ross Bay, where St. Charles Street meets Hollywood Crescent. Across the water, on San Juan Island, Dallas Mountain rises above the scene of that long-ago feud. The two form remarkable reminders of a relatively unremarkable man.

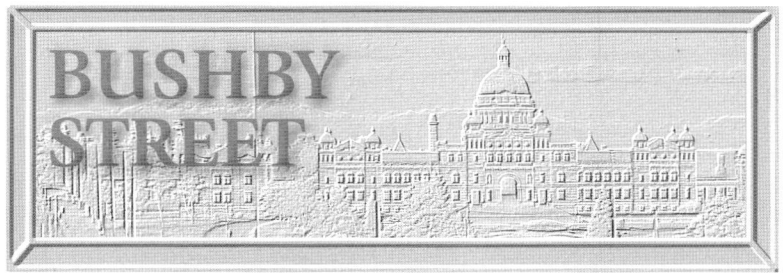

Early star of the Philharmonic

Linking Dallas Road with Memorial Crescent, just west of Ross Bay Cemetery, is a street that commemorates another James Douglas son-in-law, Arthur Thomas Bushby.

As prospective husbands go, Bushby was quite a catch. Born in London, the son of a successful merchant, he had arrived in the colony armed with a letter of introduction to Governor James Douglas from the top brass of the HBC.

It was Christmas 1858. The gold rush was in full swing and Bushby's timing was perfect. Judge Matthew Baillie Begbie, who had arrived only a few weeks earlier, was about to make his first trip to the Interior. Governor Douglas, who had been much impressed by the judge, quickly sized up young Bushby and in February 1859 appointed him Begbie's private secretary. Begbie immediately appointed him clerk of the court, assize clerk, and registrar.

Arthur Thomas and Agnes Bushby

At the end of March, the two set off for the Interior along a route Douglas had identified as being potentially suitable for a wagon road linking the gold fields with the coast. Other routes had been tried and found lacking, but Douglas felt that this one, although perhaps not the most direct, would provide the needed link between the colony's administrative headquarters and the isolated gold-mining communities.

There were two trails through the Fraser Canyon. Only one was suitable for horses and mules, and it was closed by snow. Bushby and his new boss had no option but to travel the length of the canyon on foot, accompanied by their Indian carriers. At times the going was so rough that walking was impossible and the journey became little more than a scramble over land that they later reported was fit only for man, dog, or goat.

In the gold rush days of the 1860s, Hell's Gate Canyon, 23 miles above Yale, was undoubtedly the most fearsome challenge facing explorers attempting to navigate the swift-moving Fraser river.

They followed the trail north beyond Lytton, then backtracked to Lillooet, arriving there not a moment too soon. In the lawless environment of the gold-mining camps, the hottest heads prevailed. There was friction between Natives and whites. There was friction between whites and whites. Americans easily outnumbered other whites, but there were so many different nationalities that the two justice-dispensers, intent on forming a grand jury to determine the cause of the friction, were not able to identify twelve British subjects and had to abandon the idea.

Travelling the route between Lillooet and Harrison on their way back to the coast, they passed two hot springs, which they named after two of Douglas's daughters—Agnes and Alice. Could Bushby have guessed that, before long, Agnes would become his bride?

Born in 1841 while her parents were living at Fort Vancouver, on the Columbia River, Agnes was the eighth of the Douglases' thirteen children. Cecilia, the oldest surviving daughter, was happily married to Dr. J.S. Helmcken and living next door to her parents, on Elliott Street. But during 1861 there had been disappointments: second daughter Jane had moved with her husband Alexander Dallas to Fort Garry; Alice had eloped with her father's private secretary, a fellow by the name of Charles Good. Agnes, however, seemed stable enough and was clearly delighted with her eligible new beau.

Arthur Bushby (left), pictured here with daughters Annie and Agnes, found camping with friends a welcome contrast to his earlier adventures in the B.C. Interior.

Proving himself more than capable in performance of his duties, Bushby's star continued to rise. It sparkled its brightest when he married Agnes on May 8, 1862, at Christ Church Cathedral. The wedding provided a positive focus for Agnes's parents, and they threw themselves into the celebrations. The bride, attended by seven bridesmaids, was given away by her father. The sumptuous wedding breakfast at the Hotel de France was savoured by all.

The couple lived in New Westminster and had five children. One daughter died as an infant, but the three surviving girls and a boy—Annie, Agnes, Ella, and George—were great favourites with their grandparents.

Bushby, who had a fine singing voice, continued his active involvement in the local music scene. In his early days here he had helped form the Victoria Philharmonic Society, being both its secretary and a popular performer. Judge Begbie was the society's president.

Following in his famous father-in-law's political footsteps, Bushby was a member of the Legislative Assembly from 1868 to 1870. He was registrar-general of deeds until 1870, when he became postmaster general. He also served as commissioner of savings banks in the colony, resident magistrate at New Westminster, and as county court judge on the coast and in the Interior.

A promising career was cut short when Bushby died, after a brief illness, at New Westminster in 1875. Agnes went to England and died there in 1928. Only a short street in Fairfield reminds us of their name.

FRANKLIN TERRACE

Bachelor brothers made their mark

The Victoria Philharmonic Society's first slate of officers included not only Arthur Bushby as secretary, but also two men who shared the same last name: Selim Franklin (vice-president) and Lumley Franklin (director). Once again, the Franklin brothers were united in enterprise.

The Franklins were British-born, the sons of a Liverpool banker. Successful businessmen in their own country, they travelled to the New World in the late 1840s after the discovery of California gold. Selim opened a large store in San Francisco and helped found the Chamber of Commerce there. The store did well until it was destroyed by fire. Instead of rebuilding, he and his brother focused their energies on auctioneering and real estate. When gold was discovered on the Fraser River late in 1857, the Franklins made plans to move north.

Lumley Franklin, Victoria's second mayor, and his brother Selim Franklin

It was 1858. The first Jews had arrived in Victoria in July. By fall, the first Jewish community on the British Pacific coast was firmly established. The community had its origins in England, Australia, Poland, Prussia, and Germany. Some community members mined in the gold fields; most followed their previous occupations as traders, wholesalers, and merchants. With commercial experience and sources of supply and credit at the ready, these men prospered. The first Victoria Directory, published in March 1860, featured no fewer than a dozen Jewish-owned firms.

The Franklins arrived one behind the other—Selim first, Lumley later—and before long the Yates Street premises of Franklin & Co., auctioneers and

First Jewish synagogue in the West, Congregation Emanu-El, designed by John Wright and built on the southeast corner of Blanshard and Pandora in 1863, is the oldest surviving synagogue in Canada.

land agents, was bustling. The Franklins numbered among the community's cultural mainstays. As vice-president of the Amateur Dramatic Association as well as the Victoria Philharmonic Society, Selim made his musical mark alongside his brother. Like Arthur Bushby, Lumley had enjoyed formal music studies. The Franklins sang well and frequently performed at concerts. Lumley was also a talented composer. He enjoyed setting poetry to music and once delighted an audience with his rendering of Byron's "Adieu, adieu, my native shore."

Seeing a clear advantage in his position as the only qualified auctioneer of British citizenship in these parts, Selim applied for and was appointed to the position of government auctioneer. His first auction sale of lots in New Westminster reportedly netted $90,000, which he assured mainland citizens had been earmarked by Governor James Douglas for street upgrading and other improvements. But when those improvements showed no sign of materializing, the citizenry showed its disdain for the governor by refusing to allow Selim to complete any further sales.

Selim turned his attention to politics. In 1860 he was elected to the second Legislative Assembly of Vancouver Island, triggering a tirade by fellow-electee Alfred Waddington, who complained bitterly that Franklin was incapable of taking the oath of office "on the true faith of a Christian." Chief Justice David Cameron ended a lengthy debate with a legal ruling that cited precedents for oaths being taken by Jews and other non-Christians. Franklin, the third Jew to be elected to a legislature in British North America, took his seat in the Assembly.

His political stands were not always popular. For one thing, he was vehemently opposed to the proposed union of Vancouver Island and the mainland colony, believing that the Island would suffer as a result. When the two colonies did combine in 1866, Selim resigned and returned to San Francisco.

Lumley, meanwhile, had gone from strength to strength. Unlike his brother, he favoured the union of the two colonies and was a more congenial personality to boot. In late 1865, Mayor Thomas Harris nominated him as his successor, and Franklin was duly elected second mayor of the recently incorporated city of Victoria—the first Jewish mayor of a British North American city.

Several highlights punctuated his term of office. Mid-1866 saw completion of the transatlantic cable linking Victoria with England. "No longer must we wait weeks for the post," rejoiced the mayor. "This is a day Victoria must never forget." During that same year, the city's first water pipes were laid along Yates and Government streets, and for the first time, serious attention was paid to sanitation concerns.

At the end of his mayoralty Franklin, ever the gentleman, wrote a letter of appreciation to members of his council, thanking them for their support during his term of office. Although he never sought re-election, he stayed involved with local affairs. He was delighted when the two colonies combined and when Victoria was named capital of British Columbia, and in later years was firmly committed to the concept of Confederation.

Two years after the colony joined Canada, Lumley Franklin died while in San Francisco. A decade later, Selim Franklin died there too. This is why the bachelor brothers were not laid to rest in the Jewish Cemetery on Cedar Hill Road, where other early arrivals—Davies, Friedlander, Leiser, Oppenheimer, Price, and Sylvester, to name but a few—are commemorated.

Surprisingly, considering their early presence amongst us, these pioneers are not remembered in Victoria's streets (Franklin Terrace is named after the celebrated Arctic explorer), but thanks largely to the Jewish Historical Society, their contributions to this city's early development do not go unrecognized.

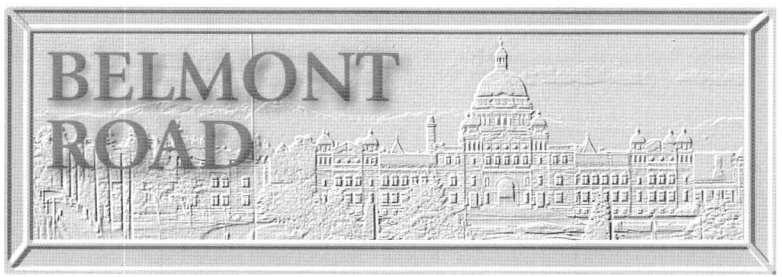

BELMONT ROAD

Governor's brother-in-law and chief justice

By the time David Cameron ruled in favour of Selim Franklin's election to the legislature, he had been chief justice for several years and was living comfortably at "Belmont," his Colwood-area home. Cameron was faring well in the new colony of Vancouver Island. Hardly surprising, since he was closely related to its governor.

Cameron was born in Perthshire, Scotland, in 1804. His attempts to make a living as a cloth merchant were unsuccessful, and by 1830 the 26-year-old was overseeing a sugar plantation in Demerara, British Guiana (now Guyana). Eight years later he bought a small property on the Essequibo, Guyana's longest river. Not long after, he married a woman called Cecilia Cowan, who had been married before and was the mother of a girl, Cecilia Eliza. Another daughter, Edith, was born in 1843.

By 1851, Cameron's business was failing and he was forced to go bankrupt. He soon rallied, however, and was able to send his stepdaughter, who had recently finished schooling in Europe, to visit the governor of Vancouver Island. James Douglas, who had paid for her education in Germany, was happy to entertain her. Cecilia's mother, after all, was his younger sister.

James had left British Guiana to attend school the year Cecilia was born and had not seen her since. He sent money to her regularly, however, and on hearing that her health was poor, suggested that she and her family move to Victoria to live.

The young Cecilia Eliza Cowan arrived first, in 1851. She lived with her uncle and aunt and made herself useful as a chaperone while her cousin—yet another Cecilia—was being courted by the handsome young Dr. John Helmcken. In December 1852 she was relieved of her duties when the Helmckens

Chief Justice David Cameron

In this view looking east from the lower portion of today's Royal Roads toward Fort Rodd Hill, "Belmont's" superb setting on a rocky slope overlooking Esquimalt Harbour can be truly appreciated. The large garden ran down to the sheltered beach where Cameron often disembarked from the naval boat that had rowed him around Macaulay Point or across from the naval base. "Belmont" was demolished near the turn of the century.

married and moved to a house of their own on the plot of land next door.

The next summer, Cecilia Eliza was joined by her mother, stepfather, and younger sister. Cecilia Senior was no stranger to this continent. In the mid-1830s she had journeyed to America in search of the husband who had deserted her. Despite journeying through several states, she never did manage to locate him, but always spoke highly of the American people and the kindness they had shown during her search.

Now she was anxious to introduce her second husband to her brother James, who had promised him a position of some importance in the new colony across the sea. The HBC, no doubt at Douglas's insistence, obliged by appointing Cameron superintendent of the coal-mining operations being developed in the Nanaimo area.

Apparently impressed by his brother-in-law, Douglas soon appointed him judge of the recently organized Supreme Court of Vancouver Island. Considering Cameron's total lack of legal experience, this was quite a startling move. Unperturbed, Douglas recommended that he be appointed chief justice, much to the chagrin of *Colonist* editor Amor De Cosmos, who knew nepotism when he saw it and later railed furiously in his newspaper against this favouring of family members.

Seemingly unfazed by the criticism levelled at him, Cameron soldiered on and to everyone's amazement managed to hold tight to his position even though his judgments were often questioned and criticized. He stepped aside in 1865, when the Island and mainland colonies were about to be combined, in order to allow someone with professional expertise to take over.

Life at "Belmont," where the Camerons presided over dinner parties and entertained their nephews and nieces, seemed idyllic. Then one day in 1858, Cecilia died. It was a terrible loss. Her niece's husband, Dr. Helmcken, later described her as being "tall, stout, dignified ... very polite and nice ... but unlike her brother, liked a joke and laughed rather pleasantly." She would be sorely missed.

Cecilia Eliza, by this time, had married William Young. After his wife's death, Cameron was so distraught that younger daughter Edith broke off her engagement to Lieut. Henry Doughty in England, saying that she felt obliged to stay with her father. Doughty, much impressed but determined to win her hand, sailed immediately to Vancouver Island. In August 1860, before witnesses David Cameron, Arthur Bushby, and James Douglas, he made Edith his bride and returned with her to England.

When Cameron retired in 1865, the *Colonist* praised his accomplishments despite "the disadvantage of a want of the requisite legal education" and declared that he had acquitted himself "to the best of his ability." He died at "Belmont" in 1872 and was buried beside his wife in the Old Burying Ground on Quadra Street.

The family is remembered in Cameron Lake west of Nanaimo, Belmont Point, Edith Point on Mayne Island, and the local street that bears the same name as their home.

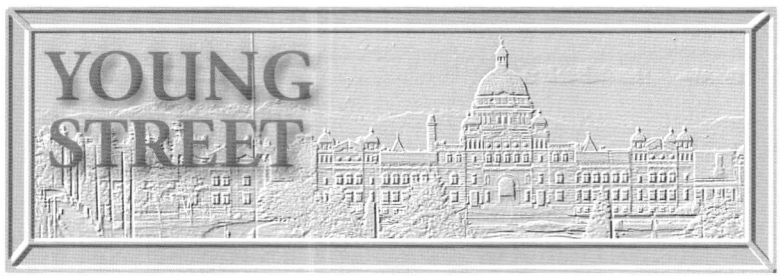

Oh to be young again ...

*I*t's not a very long street, running between Toronto and Michigan on the east side of James Bay, but in the twelve years that he lived here, the man it's named for—David Cameron's son-in-law—made quite an impression on the citizens of this town.

William Alexander George Young was born in England in 1827, the son of a captain in the Royal Navy. The younger Young followed in his father's footsteps, enlisting at the tender age of fourteen. A bright boy, he was appointed clerk to the commodore-in-chief at the age of eighteen, then served as paymaster on several ships. While the Crimean War raged around him in the Baltic, he attended to business in his usual calm, cheerful, efficient manner and was decorated for his services.

The Admiralty recommended their brightest star for administrative duties at the Foreign Office, and Young became secretary to the newly organized North American Boundary Commission.

He arrived in Victoria in June 1857. It was fourteen years since the HBC had established its new northern headquarters on the Inner Harbour, and the stockaded settlement was still the focus of activity. A few houses stood close by. Company farms fed the men at the fort. In the outlying areas, pioneering families struggled to break the land and create communities, far from the dominance of chief factor and governor James Douglas.

Fortunately for Young, he immediately made a favourable impression on his new boss, who recognized a bright young fellow when he saw one. James Douglas wasted no time in persuading him to stay. There wasn't much social life at the fort, but naval officers were always welcome, and before long Young was courting the governor's pretty young niece.

William Alexander George Young and Eliza Young

Young Street

The Youngs' Superior Street home behind the Birdcages was large, well furnished, and not far from the home of Eliza's uncle, Governor James Douglas.

Cecilia Eliza Cowan Cameron, called Eliza, had been living with her mother and stepfather at "Belmont," on the west side of Esquimalt Harbour. In 1858 several events conspired to create huge changes in the family's fortunes. Gold-seekers poured into Victoria, en route to the Fraser River. Eliza's mother died. And Eliza married the efficient young administrator who had become her Uncle James's "right-hand man." Joined in holy matrimony by HBC chaplain Edward Cridge at "Belmont" in March 1858, the Youngs set up residence on Superior Street, not far from the Douglas and Helmcken family homes. During the next decade they had three sons and three daughters. Only four of the children survived to adulthood.

In 1859, Douglas appointed the newest family member colonial secretary for the new colony of British Columbia, on the mainland. Young established a permanent residence in Victoria, which didn't go down well with mainlanders. Douglas's duties took him away more and more often, and he was only too pleased to be able to leave his son-in-law in charge. This aroused the ire of *Colonist* editor Amor De Cosmos, who was already incensed by Douglas's appointment of his wife's brother to the position of chief justice. Over the years, De Cosmos wrote caustically and at length about the governor's favouring of his own family members. Later Young also became colonial secretary for Vancouver Island and remained in

Amor De Cosmos, first editor of the British Colonist, *wrote furiously about Young and his father-in-law reaping the rewards of being related to Governor James Douglas.*

After Douglas's retirement, Governor Frederick Seymour recommended to the British government that Young be replaced as colonial secretary.

that position when the two colonies merged in 1866.

Administrative responsibilities in two colonies gave Young considerable authority—and a generous salary from both. He invested his money wisely, purchasing real estate in town, in Esquimalt, and up-Island. The Superior Street home where he lived with his wife and growing family was large and well appointed. He campaigned for membership in the Legislative Assembly, lobbying for improvements to the town, and further infuriated De Cosmos by beating him at the polls.

When Douglas retired in 1864, Young took a one-year leave of absence, and he and his family accompanied Douglas on a trip to England. During the return journey in 1865, four-year-old Cecil Young contracted diphtheria and died.

Already saddened by his personal loss, Young found British Columbia in deep financial crisis. Then he fell afoul of mainland governor Frederick Seymour, who confided to the British government that the Victoria-based Young did not inspire his confidence in connection with mainland interests.

Young was replaced. In May 1869 the Youngs auctioned off most of their possessions and sailed for England. The *Colonist* waxed eloquent about the former colonial secretary, reporting regret at his departure and assuring him that "should fate decide against his retuning here, his name will be preserved in kindly remembrance." Back in England, Young was knighted, and then appointed governor of British Guiana. He died in Accra in 1885, but his story stays with us courtesy of that short street in James Bay.

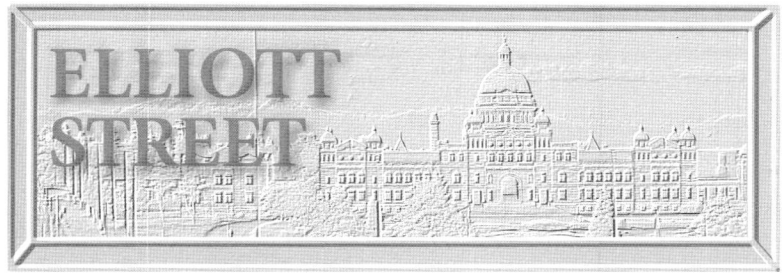

ELLIOTT STREET

"A genial, whole-souled gentleman"

You'd be forgiven for not knowing where Elliott Street is. Street guides don't show it. You can't drive along it. People say they've heard of it, but can't remember where. The fact is, Elliott Street isn't there any more. Only the middle part, beside the Royal British Columbia Museum, is still evident. The original throughway—like the man it's named after—has ceased to exist.

In later life, A.C. Elliott was a pretty powerful fellow and a great friend of Dr. J.S. Helmcken, whose house still stands on what's left of Elliott's street, but his story begins in Ireland. We believe (since records are unclear) that Andrew Charles Elliott was born there in 1828 or 1829. There's no birth certificate—only an entry in a Lillooet, B.C., census for May 1862, when he states he is 33. Like thousands of others attracted by the prospect of gold finds in B.C.'s Interior,

A.C. Elliott, his wife Mary, and daughter Mary Rachael, who in 1878 married James Douglas Jr.

Elliott left London, where he had been practising law, in early 1859. He arrived in Victoria with a letter of introduction from colonial secretary Edward Bulwer-Lytton in the summer of that same year.

By October the up-and-coming young barrister had found favour with Governor Douglas, who appointed him county court judge for Yale and Hope. The letter of commission, dated January 10, 1860, was signed by W.A.G. Young, who had made an equally favourable impression on the governor—and promptly married his favourite niece—barely two years before.

Travelling briefly to England to gather up his wife and young daughter, Elliott returned to his new appointment as assistant gold commissioner and stipendiary magistrate at Lillooet. According to Douglas, he was "active and popular" in this role. He served on the Legislative Council of the

Looking south along the picket-fenced Birdcage Walk from the corner of Elliott Street (which once joined Government and Douglas streets) toward Superior Street in the 1880s.

mainland colony of British Columbia in 1865 and 1866. When the mainland and Vancouver Island colonies united in 1867, he became high sheriff, resigned as magistrate, and shortly afterwards moved back to Victoria.

He was police magistrate for the city until 1876, when he became a member of the provincial legislature. These were exciting times. Premier George Anthony Walkem was in trouble. His government resigned a few weeks later, and Lieutenant-Governor Joseph Trutch selected Elliott to take his place. Elliott took on the triple roles of premier, attorney-general, and provincial secretary. Walkem rose again, however, and two years later Elliott—the quiet, studious, and ineffective politician—was himself out of a job when his government collapsed and he relinquished the floor to his predecessor.

Somewhat relieved to be leaving the world of politics, Elliott and his wife busied themselves with a more pressing personal venture. Their only child, Mary Rachael, was to be joined in holy matrimony with James William, only son of the late Sir James and Lady Amelia Douglas. The Rt. Reverend Bishop Edward Cridge married the young couple at the Reformed Episcopal Church, where the funeral service for Sir James had been held the year before. The bride entered the church on her father's arm, followed by eight bridesmaids. The reception at the Elliotts' home lasted until late afternoon, when Rachael and her new husband left to prepare for an early morning sailing on the *Dakota*, bound for the east.

Three years later, in 1881, Mary Elliott died suddenly and unexpectedly and was laid to rest in a brick vault not far from Sir James Douglas's own at Ross Bay Cemetery. She was only 47. Elliott, who had been away in London when she died, was much distressed. He continued to travel, but when he was in Victoria, he spent more time with his daughter and son-in-law at their Michigan Street home.

He was not long for this world. Plagued by what the *Daily Colonist* described as "neuralgia of the eyes and other disorders of a painful nature," he sought relief in California. His condition did not improve. His daughter visited him often, and on April 9, 1889, he died there in her arms, at the age of 60. In accordance with his wishes, she brought him back to Victoria and buried him next to his beloved wife, her mother. Reporting his death, the *Colonist* ignored his political bumblings, saying instead that he administered justice with a fearless hand and was a "genial, whole-souled gentleman of generous impulses … brave to a fault."

His son-in-law survived him by only two years. His daughter lived longer, but no record of her death has been found.

So ended the Elliott line. As did Elliott Street, which disappeared during the mid-1970s construction of an addition to the Royal B.C. Museum. The Douglas home had been razed some 60 years before. Today, all that's left is sturdy, wood-framed Helmcken House, which still stands where it was built in 1852 by the doctor who became Andrew Charles Elliott's friend.

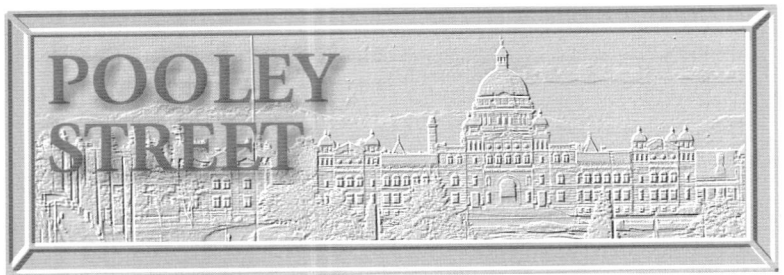

Pick and shovel paved his path to parliament

One of the pallbearers at A.C. Elliott's 1899 funeral was a fellow who in the early days shared his fascination for the gold fields, and later shared his passion for politics.

Charles Edward Pooley was born at Upwood, in Huntingdonshire, England, in 1845. Armed with a grammar school education, he was only seventeen when he arrived in Victoria in 1862. Like Elliott, he headed for the Cariboo. Their paths likely didn't cross. While Elliott was assistant gold commissioner, Pooley was at the business end of a gold-digger's shovel. He didn't strike it rich, but he did make one very important contact in the gold fields—Judge Matthew Baillie Begbie.

Reading his letters of introduction and seeing the young fellow's potential, Begbie advised him to study law. Pooley left the Interior and moved down to New Westminster. There he worked hard cutting cordwood, laying out gardens, and digging drains. In 1863 he joined the public service. Appointed clerk in the Department of the Attorney-General and clerk to the Registrar-General, he quickly rose through the ranks, becoming Acting Registrar of British Columbia, then Registrar of the mainland portion of B.C., and eventually Registrar of the Supreme Court. He travelled extensively throughout the province with Judge Begbie, who was knighted by Queen Victoria in 1874.

Life was good. In 1869, Pooley had married Elizabeth Wilhelmina, the only daughter of William Fisher, at St. Paul's Naval Garrison Church. Elizabeth's father brought his family to Victoria in 1864. Guns were fired as they stepped ashore—it was Queen Victoria's birthday, but William Fisher took the royal salute as just another positive omen for his family's new start here.

The Hon. C.E. Pooley in the 1890s. Pooley was president of the executive council during John Robson's term as premier of B.C. from 1890 to 1892.

As one of only three young ladies in Esquimalt at that time, Lizzie Fisher was much in demand at naval picnics, parties, and dances, but it was at a Governor's Ball in New Westminster that she met the tall, handsome young man who charmed his way into her heart.

The Pooleys' three sons, Tom (top), Harry (front), and Charlie. Harry became his father's partner and followed him into politics.

Elizabeth Fisher Pooley rasied six children and resided as matriarch of Frenhill for over half a century.

Charles and Lizzie Pooley were among the first to be married at St. Paul's, and their wedding—attended by naval officers as well as family and friends—was the largest Esquimalt had known. The Pooleys lived in New Westminster, then returned to Esquimalt and their new home just off Esquimalt Road on Lampson Street. "Fernhill" was surrounded by parkland, whose shoulder-high ferns gave rise to its name. The view south across Esquimalt Road toward the Olympic Mountains, over the green meadows of what had once been Donald Macaulay's Viewfield Farm, was magnificent. There wasn't another house or a fence in sight.

Esquimalt Road was always busy. In the early days, mail and passenger steamers from California arrived once every two weeks, and throngs of people filled the road on their way to and from Victoria. It was three miles from the dock to the city. There was always the stage, if it wasn't packed to overflowing, but most people walked the whole distance and thought nothing of it. After a long day in his Victoria office, Pooley loved to hunt down by Macaulay

Point before walking home through the woods.

The Pooleys had four daughters (one of whom died in infancy) and three sons. He was an avid cricketer and taught his children the ins and outs of the game so that they could report the progress of any he could not personally attend.

In 1877 Pooley was admitted to the bar. He resigned his post as Registrar and went into partnership with A. E. B. Davie, who would later become premier of B.C. Ten years later, Pooley waded into the political fray. Elected to the legislature for Esquimalt, he soon became Speaker of the House, and in 1889 he was made president of the Executive Council. He held that position in the cabinet of premiers John Robson, Theodore Davie (whom he had proposed for premier rather than assume the position himself), and John Turner. When Turner relinquished the reins of office in 1898, Pooley retired.

Aside from his professional and political activities, Pooley was also involved in many business and commercial enterprises, including the Colonist Printing and Publishing Co. and the Esquimalt Waterworks. A keen cricketer still, he enjoyed good health until a few years after the turn of the century, when his vision began to fail. He sought treatment from a world-famous oculist in Germany, and on his return was able, reported the *Colonist*, "to again recognize and greet his old friends with his accustomed smile."

It was a reprieve, of sorts, but the end wasn't far away. Gradually he weakened, to the point where he had to relinquish all professional duties. And then, after several weeks of increasing illness, Charles Pooley took a turn for the worse. He died at his home on March 28, 1912, unaware that Harry, his son and partner in practice, had continued the family tradition by being elected that very same day to represent his father's old constituency of Esquimalt.

Pooley was buried at Ross Bay Cemetery, later joined there by Lizzie, who had lived on at "Fernhill" until her death in 1932. Their grave, guarded by a white marble angel, and Pooley Place, at the other end of Lampson Street from the family home, remind us of these early Esquimalt pioneers.

MYSTIC LANE

Who's afraid of Julia Booth?

There are few more intriguing stories than the one set in the wooded area just east of the University of Victoria, where a young girl lost her life more than a hundred years ago.

When the first Hudson's Bay Company settlers arrived at Fort Victoria, Cadboro Bay was the site of an Indian encampment. Natives used the cedar trees in the forest at the east end of the bay to make their canoes. In early July they paddled across to the San Juan Islands for salmon fishing. By September they had stored enough dried food and grease to see them through the winter. Returning to their camp on the south side of Cadboro Bay, they followed the rituals of early fall—dancing, feasting, picking berries, burying salmon eggs. Then they travelled overland to the Inner Harbour and the Gorge.

They followed one of two routes—along present-day Cadboro Bay Road and Fort Street to the vicinity of Roderick Finlayson's first house, west of Douglas Street and north of the fort; or along what is now Cedar Hill Cross Road to the Gorge, up to Portage Inlet, and across to Esquimalt Harbour. They may also have paddled to the Inner Harbour along a chain of swamps and creeks that led to the eastern end of James Bay, where the Church of Our Lord stands today.

The trails and inner waterways were used in the winter months, when the storm-tossed seas made it too dangerous to paddle along the coastline. It was a necessary journey, a hunting trip to gather ducks, geese, and deer that would help feed the many hungry mouths at Cadboro Bay.

When Father J. Bolduc, the priest who accompanied James Douglas's group to Vancouver Island in 1843, walked to Cadboro Bay, he found more than 500 Natives, who gathered to greet the stranger in their midst. They were eager to share their stories with the new arrivals. Many tales were told, but few were more tantalizing than the one about a crystal-clear stream of water—the amazing Mystic Spring.

The water apparently had its source far from the bay, at the northern end of what we now know as Mystic Vale. The stream flowed down through a ravine bordered by tall trees, shrubs, flowering plants, and ferns, disappeared underground, and reappeared as if by magic as a spring at the roots of a huge maple tree, only to disappear again on its route through open fields to the bay.

The spring, said the Natives, had magical properties. The maple tree was its guardian angel. If anyone chopped the tree down, the water would stop flowing. In the meantime, a

More than three decades after Julia Booth's death, the Cadboro Bay Beach Hotel (pictured, right foreground, in the early 1900s and since demolished) stood on the still sparsely populated Cadboro Bay waterfront.

woman looking into the spring's clear waters when the moon was full would see the face of the man who loved her. If a man looked into the spring, a woman's face would appear.

Over the ensuing years, the young people of Fort Victoria flocked to the secluded pond alongside Mystic Creek. At first skeptical, many became believers. In 1862, one girl fainted at the sight of the "fearful" face she said stared at her from beneath the surface. Six years later, another girl lost her life to the legend.

Julia Booth's story would be told almost 40 years later, in a book written and published in 1904 by former newspaper editor and Speaker of the legislature D.W. Higgins. In *The Mystic Spring and Other Tales of Western Life*, Higgins described how eighteen-year-old Julia went to the area one April evening in 1868, not with friends, but by herself. She seemed cheerful enough to the local resident who gave her directions to the spring, but a young Native boy would later tell how he had seen her rocking to and fro as she sobbed uncontrollably at the water's edge. No one knows what happened next, but one thing is certain—the next morning her lifeless body was found. Some say she was floating in the pool. Others say she drowned in the sea at Cadboro Bay.

Victorians were shocked. Edgar Fawcett was more horrified than most. Years later, in his *Reminiscences of Old Victoria*, he recalled that he had known Julia well—they were the same age and had met many times at dances, picnics, and other festivities. When he heard of her death, he remembered meeting her on Cadboro Bay Road and was horrified to realize that he was probably the last white person to see her alive.

Did she fall? Was she pushed? Did the spirits reach out and pull her into her watery grave? Who can solve the mystery of Mystic Spring?

Next Halloween, go to the southeast corner of the University of Victoria campus or to the southwest end of Hobbs Road and wander through the lush greenness of Mystic Vale. Be careful as you follow the muddy, maple leaf-covered path through the tall trees. Be mindful of the deer, rabbits, owls, eagles, and bats that surround you. And beware the ghost of Julia Booth.

The deceptively peaceful woods and water at Cadboro Bay will forever preserve the secret of Julia Booth's demise. Some of Mystic Vale's mature, second-growth trees are estimated to be at least 500 years old.

SHAKESPEARE STREET

No poetry for the postmaster

More than 50 years after he attended the funeral of schoolmate Julia Booth, Edgar Fawcett was pallbearer at another funeral—this one for fellow retiree Noah Shakespeare.

Shakespeare had led a long and interesting life. He was born in Brierly Hills, Staffordshire, in January 1839, the son of Noah and Hannah Shakespeare. They claimed descent from the Bard of Avon himself, who had died at the city of Stratford more than 200 years earlier.

William Shakespeare, son of a glover in the city of Stratford, was well educated and enjoyed a childhood without hardship. Times were tougher for his nineteenth-century namesake. At the age of eight, Noah was working fourteen hours a day, six days a week in a chain shop. Two years later he went to school for a while to gain the education that would serve him well in later life. Then it was back to work in his teens, with the prospect of a lifetime of hard work in one of Staffordshire's huge mills.

Shakespeare decided to tip the scales in his own favour by developing gold fever. For a recently married 23-year-old with few prospects in his own hometown, the lure of the mines must have seemed like light at the end of a tunnel. In August 1862 he boarded the *Robert Lowe* and set sail for the new colony far across the sea.

The weather was foul and the passage delayed. By the time the *Robert Lowe* sailed into Esquimalt Harbour it was mid-January 1863. In a *Victoria Daily Times* interview more than 50 years later, Shakespeare recounted his dismay at learning that landing on Sundays was against the rule. Passengers would not be allowed ashore until Monday.

Noah and Elizabeth Shakespeare

Four and a half months without a Sunday service was plenty enough for the avid young churchgoer. Shakespeare went to the captain and was given permission to disembark. Following the rough, winding road from Esquimalt, he located the Pandora Street Methodist Church. He attended the midmorning service, bought himself a hearty lunch, then kept his word to the *Robert Lowe*'s captain by trudging back along the muddy trail to spend one last night on board.

The next morning the *Emily Harris* transported the *Robert Lowe*'s passengers to Victoria. Like many others who learned of the uncertainty of finding a fortune in the gold fields, Shakespeare decided to try his luck elsewhere. Coal seemed a better bet than gold. The *Emily Harris* was Nanaimo-bound. When it pulled out of Victoria Harbour, Shakespeare was aboard. Signing up with coalmaster and mine manager Robert Dunsmuir, he worked two shifts a day, earning $2 per shift. Soon he could afford to send for the wife he had married in England in 1859.

With Elizabeth and their oldest child at his side, Shakespeare worked at the mine for almost a year and a half, then returned to Victoria to pursue yet another career—photography. Originally hired to help in the shop, he became so proficient that a year later he was left in sole charge while his employer took a trip to England. Then he found a job with Amor De Cosmos, editor of the brand-new *Standard*. Shakespeare worked the hand-press, then became one of two newspaper deliverymen. Victoria was still small enough that each man

Just around the corner from the post office where Shakespeare worked, the Customs House stood proudly on the west side of Wharf Street. The shoreline in the background, in turn a Native village, railway yard, and industrial site, now features a hotel and condominiums.

could deliver papers to half of the town.

He went back to photography for a while, then dabbled in real estate. But it was politics that pleased him the most. He served as alderman, then as Victoria's fourteenth mayor. It was 1882. In the fall of that year, when the Marquis of Lorne, Governor General of Canada, and his wife, Queen Victoria's daughter Princess Louise, came to visit, Mayor Shakespeare was honoured to be their host.

At the end of his mayoral term, he moved to Ottawa and a seat in the House of Commons. He served until 1887, then resigned and returned to Victoria to take up the position of

Looking north across the harbour from Belleville Street in the late 1890s, the post office on the corner of Wharf and Government streets looms above boathouses at the foot of the slope near where Ship Point and the Visitor Information Centre are today. Half-hidden by the post office building, the huge Weiler Bros. sign on their showroom at Government and Courtney advertises "Furniture, carpets, wallpaper, complete house furnishings." Top left in the picture is the distinctive peak of the Rattenbury-designed Bank of Montreal, erected in 1897 on the corner of Government and Bastion Square.

postmaster. The post office was at the core of Victoria's business community. Shakespeare's job was an important one and he took it seriously.

He was equally serious about his community activities. Over the years he was president of the Mechanics Institute, the YWCA, and the provincial branch of the Sunday School Association, and was heavily involved with Bible study work. In sharp contrast to these church-based endeavours were his tireless efforts to curb Chinese immigration. In the 1870s he was president of an anti-Chinese society. Later, while a Member of Parliament, he helped secure the immigration restriction law that was passed in 1886.

In 1913, Shakespeare resigned from the post office and prepared to enjoy the rest of his years with his wife and the surviving four of their eight children. In May 1921 he died at his Dunedin Street home. Fellow retiree Edgar Fawcett helped carry his coffin into the Centennial Church, then accompanied it to Ross Bay. Three hundred years after the poet Shakespeare was laid to rest in Stratford-upon-Avon, his lesser-known namesake was buried at Ross Bay. Several blocks north of the cemetery, a street sign reminds us of his name.

A deeply religious man, Shakespeare attended—and was buried from—Centennial United Church (pictured in 1891) on Gorge Road.

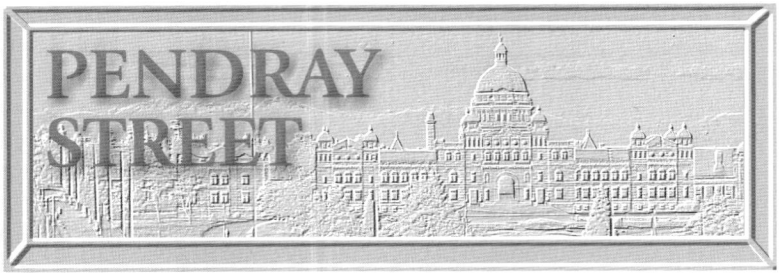

The man who cleaned up

By the early 1880s, the area north of today's Empress Hotel was the site of an enterprising venture established by Victoria's cleaning product king. W.J. Pendray's soap factory was on one side of James Bay. His home was on the other.

William Joseph Pendray had come a long way from the home in Cornwall, England, where he was born in 1845. Hearing of the fortunes to be made in California, he journeyed there in the 1860s to stake his claim. It didn't take him long to realize he would never make his fortune earning three dollars a day. He packed up and travelled via Victoria to the Cariboo. A few years later he had made enough money to retire to England. But the New World had left its mark. In the early 1870s, his fortunes dissipated in unsuccessful investments, he returned to America, this time to Nevada. Soon he had made enough money to bring himself north once again.

The Victoria of 1875 was a very different place to the town he had first seen more than a decade before. It was now the capital of British Columbia, which was a province of Canada. The HBC fort, long since demolished, had been replaced by commercial buildings. Businesses lined the length of Government Street. Dozens of merchants provided for all the citizens' needs, except one—the wherewithal to keep clean. Pendray decided to relieve Victorians of the obligation to import soap by making his own in a factory close to the north end of the wooden bridge that crossed the water at James Bay's eastern end. Pendray's soap works at Humboldt and Douglas streets backed onto the bay, contributing to the stench that sickened local residents.

According to the 1882–83 B.C. Directory, Pendray's White Swan soap plant used 3,000 pounds of tallow per week to make 10,000 pounds of different types of cleansers. Coarse, antiseptic soap was designed to help men in the gold-mining towns rid themselves of lice. Twelve kinds of ordinary household soap were complemented by toilet soaps of every scent and colour.

In 1877, his business well established, Pendray was ready to take a bride. He had proposed to Amelia Jane Carthew, also a native of Cornwall, two years before. Now she sailed from Liverpool to join her future husband. One month and two days later she stepped ashore at Esquimalt. The two were married the next day and took up residence in a house on Douglas Street, near today's Crystal Garden. Over the ensuing years they had four sons. One—Carl—became Victoria's 33rd mayor.

In the 1890s, Pendray's British Columbia Soap Works stood on the corner of Douglas and Humboldt streets, draining its soap-making residues into the muddy waters of James Bay. By 1908 the factory was gone, and the mudflats had given way to the elegant Empress Hotel.

Pictured from Laurel Point in the 1940s, "Loretto Hall" stood proudly on the corner of Belleville and St. John (now Pendray) streets. Today it is dwarfed by a hotel on the street behind.

In 1896, William Joseph and Amelia Pendray posed on the steps of their Belleville Street home with sons Herbert, Roy, Ernest, and Carl. Ernest (seated, right) died in a 1909 horse-and-buggy accident just a few yards from "Loretto Hall"'s front gate. Carl (right) eventually became Victoria's 33rd mayor.

Pendray was forward-looking in more ways than one. In 1877, when B.C.'s first telephone exchange opened for business in a small building in Thomas Trounce's alley, Pendray's soap works was the first to be connected—to a clothing store several blocks away at Government and Yates. The equipment, brought up from San Francisco, comprised a one-piece receiver and transmitter. After talking, the instrument was taken from the lips and placed to the ear so that the person on the other end of the line could be heard. It was truly one of the wonders of Victoria.

After moving twice and wearying of the hustle and bustle of downtown Victoria, the Pendrays built a new home for themselves on their property at the far side of James Bay. It was designed in the American Queen Anne style and completed in 1897. A many-sided tower, three stories high, afforded magnificent views of the harbour and the new Parliament Buildings rising on the grassy slope to the east.

There were frescoed walls and ceilings—unusual in a private residence at that time—and leaded glass in the doors and windows. There was a library and a billiard room and lots of places where the Pendray boys could play. Outside, there was a tennis court, an electric fountain, and gardens featuring their father's latest hobby—topiary. Trees and shrubs were trimmed into striking, sometimes grotesque, shapes. Pendray's careful creations formed the focus for many a family's Sunday afternoon walk.

The new home was spacious, gracious, and best of all, it was only two blocks from the plant that by 1899 housed the soap works and a recently acquired operation—the British America Paint Company, or Bapco. Canadian Pacific had bought the old downtown site. Eventually CP drained the mudflats and replaced them with a beautiful new hotel, set back from the causeway that allowed Government Street to continue on into James Bay.

The boys joined their father in the soap and paint business. The stage seemed set for long-lasting success. But in 1909 the happiness of the Pendray home was shattered by the sudden death of oldest son Ernest, killed when he was thrown from a horse-drawn buggy almost on his parents' Belleville Street doorstep. Three years later W.J. too was gone, victim of a freak accident at his own soap plant.

Lever Brothers bought the soap works and moved it to Vancouver. Many years later, Bapco Paint followed. Amelia lived on at the family home until her own death, at the age of 87, in 1937. She and William are buried together at Ross Bay.

Bapco is long gone, leaving in its place on Laurel Point a fine hotel and condominiums. Only a short street—once called St. John, now Pendray—and the carefully restored house and garden at 309 Belleville remind us of the family that reigned supreme over the northwestern tip of the peninsula known as James Bay.

The grounds of "Loretto Hall" were full of bushes trimmed into strange and grotesque shapes. William Pendray loved his topiary garden, rising early in the morning to wield his garden shears before going to work. His efforts were appreciated by the never-ending stream of people who perambulated past his property on Sunday afternoons.

RATTENBURY PLACE

He had designs on Victoria

On the east side of Mount Tolmie there's a short road with a long story behind it. The story begins in England, with the birth of a boy who was destined to spend more than half his life half a world away. Much has been written about this man over the years. His life was remarkable; his death even more so. Decades after his demise, his name lingers on in the city he helped design.

Francis Mawson Rattenbury, the second son of John and Mary Anne Rattenbury, was born near Leeds, Yorkshire, in 1867. Finishing school and then college with not the slightest urge to join the business pursuits of the men on his mother's side of the family, he chose instead to follow in his father's footsteps. Both were more inclined toward art than industry, and at the age of 18, the younger Rattenbury moved to the city of Bradford to join his uncle's architectural firm.

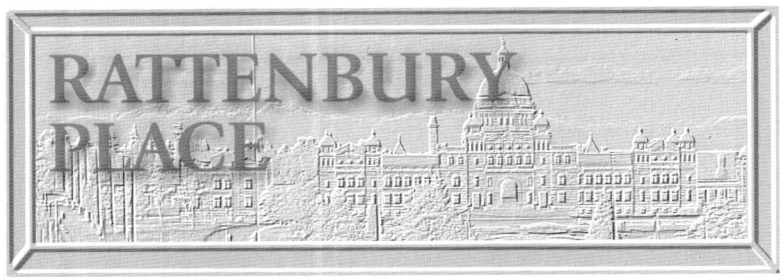

Francis Mawson and Florence Rattenbury

For six years Rattenbury learned his chosen trade. Then, frustrated by the lack of opportunities and anxious to find an appropriate outlet for his ambitions, he set his sights on a place far from the land of his birth. In 1892 he sailed for Canada's West Coast. He was 24 years old.

The Vancouver that awaited him was challenge enough for any ambitious young man. It had grown by leaps and bounds in the six years since its incorporation as a city destined to be the western terminus of Canada's transcontinental railway line. The small, higgledy-piggledy settlement of the 1860s had become a neatly laid-out townsite with a large population, its long, straight streets lined with fine buildings.

Even though the first rush of building activity had slowed, Rattenbury sensed opportunities galore. He designed a home for German-born Gustav Roedde, Vancouver's first

Rattenbury Place

Looking every inch the seat of provincial government, Rattenbury's Parliament Buildings rose majestically behind one of the last Birdcages to bite the dust.

printer, on a rise overlooking English Bay in the heart of the city's West End. Other successful bids would surely have followed ... had his attentions not been diverted by a tantalizing opportunity across the water.

The city of Victoria was looking for someone to design a grand new headquarters for the government of British Columbia. H.O. Tiedemann's "Birdcages," erected in 1859, had outlived their usefulness. They were too small, too difficult to heat, and too shabby to impress visitors. The government held a competition to replace them, and architects were invited to submit their entries.

Rising to this unexpected challenge, Rattenbury confidently put pencil to paper. No matter that his sole claim to architectural fame was his contribution to the design of two municipal buildings in his native Yorkshire. His belief in his own largely untested ability was unwavering. Required to submit under a nom de plume, and guessing that local entrants would be favoured, he signed himself "B.C. Architect" and moved to Victoria in order to establish a credible presence there. His ruse paid off. In the spring of 1893 he learned that he had beaten out 66 other entrants and won the competition to design the new Legislative Buildings.

Victorians watched with amazement as the magnificent stone structure arose behind the birdcage-like buildings on the shore of James Bay. Completed in 1898, this masterpiece—

In 1908, the original centre portion of Rattenbury's Empress Hotel stood in solitary splendour behind the newly constructed causeway that replaced the James Bay Bridge. Just a few years later (below), the causeway was lined by landscaped gardens and featured a ceremonial arch.

In happier days, Rattenbury posed outside his Oak Bay waterfront home (now Glenlyon School).

unlike any edifice Rattenbury had worked on or even encountered in his short professional life—signalled the start of a career that would span three decades and the whole province of British Columbia. Locally, his work on buildings such as the Bank of Montreal, Government House, and the Empress Hotel cemented his reputation as a designer with vision and verve.

There were hiccups along the way. Brilliant, but not a team player, Rattenbury rarely lived by the rules. Over the years there were assertions of professional wrongdoing, bitter accusations, and broken promises. Never at a loss for words, Rattenbury railed at those who challenged him, denied every accusation, justified every move.

His personal life was a shambles. Married to Florence, whom he no longer loved, he sought solace in the arms of a beautiful temptress 30 years his junior. Florrie Rattenbury was solid and respectable; Alma was anything but. Frivolous, flirty, and as focused on her own needs as her new beau, she accepted with alacrity Rattenbury's invitation to establish herself as Florrie's replacement. It was a move that would affect—and eventually end—the lives of all three.

Florrie reluctantly agreed to a divorce and died soon afterward. Rattenbury and Alma legalized their union in marriage and prepared to rejoin the social scene, but Victorians were not amused and made no attempt to welcome

Francis Rattenbury and small son Frank enjoyed many a carriage ride along the leafy Oak Bay lanes.

the prodigal son back into the fold. Shunned by the same society that had once welcomed him with open arms, Rattenbury left his two grown children to their own devices and took Alma, her son from a previous marriage, and their own infant son back to England.

Removed from any connection with his famous past, he became depressed. Although he contemplated suicide, he didn't die by his own hand. It was George Percy Stoner, Alma's young lover, who brought things to a head by bludgeoning Rattenbury to death in a jealous rage. Stoner was arrested and sentenced to death, but was reprieved after Alma, unable to contemplate living without him, took her own life a few days later.

It was the end of an era, the last chapter in the story of Francis Mawson Rattenbury, architect of Victoria and ultimately, one might say, of his own demise. All that remains are the magnificent buildings he designed and a short city street that, like the man it's named after, starts out with promise, then comes to a disappointing—and very dead—end.

MACLURE ROAD

The real B.C. Architect

Rattenbury may have claimed the title when he entered the competition to design the Legislative Buildings, but another man—Samuel Maclure—was the real "B.C. Architect." Rattenbury came here from England; Maclure was born in B.C.

Older than Rattenbury by some seven years, Maclure was born at a momentous time in the province's history. It was 1860—just two years since Queen Victoria had chosen the name British Columbia for her new colony west of the Rockies, and one year since Queensborough (as New Westminster was then called) had been chosen as the new colony's capital.

Samuel was the first white boy-child born to pioneers on the mainland's Matsqui Prairie. His father, John Maclure, was a native of Scotland, a Royal Engineer who met his future bride in Ireland and married her a few years before volunteering his services in the new land across the sea. In 1858 Martha Maclure undertook the long, arduous voyage around Cape Horn to join her husband. John must have been delighted to see his wife and two young daughters, and even more delighted when on April 11, 1860, their first son was born.

By the time the newest Maclure entered the world, the gold fever that had flared along the banks of the Fraser River was prepared to rage on up into the Cariboo. When young Sam was two, his father was helping to construct the Cariboo Wagon Road, and the town of Barkerville boasted the largest population north of San Francisco.

At the age of four, Sam probably wasn't aware that Sir James Douglas, recently knighted by Queen Victoria, had retired from public office. At six, Sam doubtless didn't realize that British Columbia and Vancouver Island were now one colony. But at 11, when British Columbia

Samuel and Daisy Maclure

A keen artist, Maclure painted this picture of the wreck of the SS San Pedro *on Brotchie Ledge in 1892.*

entered Confederation and became the sixth province in the Dominion of Canada, he would have been out there cheering with the rest.

The younger Maclure decided to study art when he left school, and in 1884 he travelled to Philadelphia. There he became aware of two things—a growing interest in architecture, and a dwindling income with which to pay for his education. Returning to B.C., he worked as a telegraph operator at Duncan to support himself while he studied at home to be an architect. It was on one of his regular trips to Victoria that he met his future wife.

In church one Sunday, the 28-year-old Maclure was smitten by the beautiful 18-year-old Margaret Catherine Simpson, or Daisy as she was called. The attraction was mutual, and before long, Maclure asked for Daisy's hand in marriage. To his dismay, her parents refused. The age difference was too great, said her minister stepfather, and his achievements too small. Daring and undaunted, the young couple hatched a plot. Maclure sailed for Vancouver. A few days later, an old woman dressed in black, walking with the aid of a cane, made her way slowly to the dock. When she reached the mainland, Maclure and his "old lady" were married. The newlyweds settled in New Westminster, and by the time they returned to Victoria in 1892 with their young daughter, all was forgiven.

Between 1887 and 1892, Maclure worked with two different firms in New Westminster, and by 1892 he was ready to open his own practice in Victoria. At first he designed bungalow-style homes. Then in 1893 came a breakthrough—a commission to design business premises for the firm of Robert Ward & Co. The Temple Building, in the 500-block Fort Street, survives to this day as the only known example of Maclure's commercial activities.

The Temple Building was Maclure's first major independent commission and is his only commercial structure still standing. Built on the 500-block of Fort Street in 1893, it features sandstone combined with red pressed brick. Strange faces peer out from the centre of terracotta floral shapes

Over the years Maclure designed other commercial buildings, schools, hotels, even a children's hospital. But it was people's homes that pleased him the most. Stone and half-timbered plaster exteriors, huge entry halls, high-beamed ceilings, and leaded glass windows became Maclure trademarks. Spacious, light, and airy, his designs lent themselves to entertaining on a grand scale, a feature of Victoria society in those turn-of-the-century days. By then he had established himself firmly in the minds of Victorians as the architect of choice when it came to large-but-liveable homes.

The Maclures lived first in James Bay, then Oak Bay, and eventually built a house not far from Rattenbury's waterfront home. Though very different characters, the two men became friendly. In 1903 Maclure worked alongside Rattenbury on the design of the new Government House. That same year he opened a Vancouver office with partner Cecil Fox. This successful and congenial partnership thrived until Fox's untimely death on the battlefields of France in 1915.

Maclure was a kindly fellow, literate and artistic, an amateur photographer who loved

Maclure's largest residential commission—Hatley Park—was designed in 1910 to be a palatial home and country retreat for former lieutenant-governor James Dunsmuir and his family. Today it is the picturesque centrepiece for Royal Roads University.

poetry. His watercolour paintings were as delicate and gentle as the man himself. In his work he had an acute eye for detail. His houses' interiors combined beauty and practicality, creating places of comfort that clearly reflected the characters of their inhabitants. To Maclure, the outside was as important as the inside. He believed the most beautiful house was the one set in equally beautiful grounds, and an architect should be able to design a garden to complement the dwelling.

He may have had no formal training, but his was a formidable talent and his work did not go unnoticed in other parts of the world. French and English architectural magazines commented favourably on it and credited him with setting high standards to which others could aspire. Many Maclure homes have disappeared or been altered almost beyond recognition, but many more have survived in Greater Victoria and throughout the province of British Columbia, as well as in Edmonton, Toronto, and south of the border.

Maclure died in 1929 after a short illness. According to his wishes, his ashes were scattered in Matsqui, the pioneer community where he had lived as a boy. Ten years later, Daisy too was gone, mourned by their three daughters.

Amazingly, although the city of his birth has honoured its native son by naming a street after him, Victoria has somehow managed to miss that opportunity. There's a Maclure Street in New Westminster. High time we had one here, don't you think?

And if Victoria's McClure Street isn't named after Samuel Maclure (note the different spelling), then who *is* it named after?

Robert John LeMesurier McClure was involved in the search for Sir John Franklin's expedition, missing in the Arctic since 1848. In 1850 the British Admiralty sent two ships to look for the party. Marie Elliott told their story in the *Times Colonist* "Islander" of July 13, 1980.

One ship—the *Enterprise*—was under the command of Captain Richard Collinson. The other—the *Investigator*—was captained by R.J.L. McClure. Despite strict instructions from the Admiralty to stay together, the two vessels quickly lost touch. Collinson's was the faster sailing ship, but it was McClure who reached Alaska first and penetrated deep into the ice-pack. Collinson, arriving too late to follow, was forced to winter in Hong Kong. The next spring, two searches were underway: one for Franklin and one for McClure, who, unknown to Collinson, had become permanently trapped by the ice. Another group rescued McClure and his crew in 1853. McClure returned to England in 1854 and claimed that he had discovered the western half of the elusive Northwest Passage.

A year later, Collinson sailed back into Plymouth Harbour. News of troubles with his men had preceded him. The Admiralty, not wanting to make his difficulties public, responded by crediting McClure with the discovery of *a* (though not necessarily *the*) Northwest Passage, and awarded him 10,000 pounds. McClure was posted to China. Collinson stayed in England and was eventually knighted in 1875.

McClure Street is right next to Collinson and is nestled amongst a series of streets—Cook, Vancouver, Richardson, Humboldt, and Meares—that commemorate men who made exhilarating voyages of discovery at some point in time.

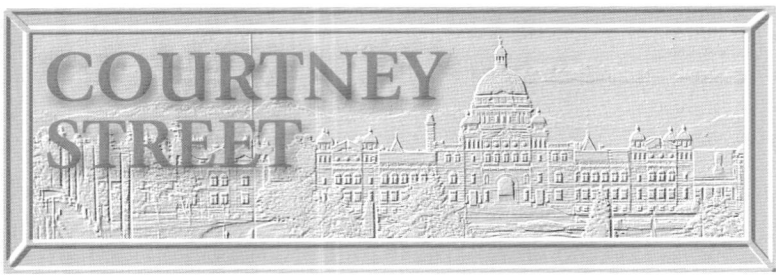

The solicitor and the man of the sea

*I*t takes some nifty detective work to track down the origins of some Victoria streets. Changes were made willy-nilly, it seems, and total accuracy wasn't always a major concern. One downtown street that's been a victim of name misspelling is Courtney Street. Some say it was named after a sea captain; others say it was a solicitor. Who is right? Well, let's take a look at the fellow who arrived here first.

Walbran's *British Columbia Coast Names* tells us that Captain George William Conway Courtenay sailed to these parts in 1846, at the tail end of a long and distinguished career. Forty years before, Captain Courtenay had served as midshipman aboard HMS *Amazon*. He was at the capture of the French frigates *Marengo* and *Belle Poule*, and served on shore with the naval brigade on the north coast of Spain. Made lieutenant in 1814, he served on the *Cyrene* in 1822 and took part in an attack on a slave factory on the African coast. By 1824 he was commanding the *Owen Glendower* and was made captain in 1828.

Two decades later he sailed aboard the Navy vessel *Constance* to Esquimalt. It's said that the *Constance* was the first of Her Majesty's ships to sail into Esquimalt Harbour, but the *Pandora* probably anchored there in 1846 while its crew surveyed the harbour, two years before Courtenay arrived. At more than 2,000 tons and with 50 guns, the *Constance* was a fine-looking frigate. It was one of many on this station before the fledgling Fort Victoria, established in 1843, became the HBC's official northern headquarters.

Henry Classon and Mary Jane Courtney.

In a letter to William Miller, British consul in Honolulu, dated July 25, 1848, Courtenay stated that it had taken the *Constance* 26 days to sail up the coast from San Francisco. He said

John Turnstall Haverfield's painting shows HMS Constance, *reputedly the first Royal Navy vessel to sail into Esquimalt Harbour in 1848.*

that the HBC settlement called Fort Victoria had 300 acres under tillage, a dairy farm and 80 cows, other cattle, and 24 brood mares, along with "30 people of all descriptions," all under the superintendence of "a civil but hard Scot named Finlaison [sic]."

Courtenay was on this station for only six weeks. He sailed for San Francisco at the beginning of September, then on to Callao, Mazatlan, Valparaiso, and eventually, in 1849, back home to England. That same year, the HBC leased the whole of Vancouver Island from the Crown, and James Douglas earmarked Esquimalt for agricultural development. Soon, the cove named after Courtenay's ship formed part of the southern border of Thomas Skinner's 600-acre Constance Cove Farm. By that time Captain Courtenay was off on another adventure. In 1861 he was made vice-admiral and he died in 1863.

Meanwhile, a young fellow with a similar-sounding name was making his mark here. Henry Classon Courtney was born in Dublin in 1836. He studied law and started legal practice in 1859. Still in his twenties when he sailed across the sea to North America, he arrived when Victoria was also still a young town.

In early 1862, while the town readied itself for incorporation as the City of Victoria, the *Colonist* reported that Courtney had been

The Volunteer Rifle Corps Band played at many an official celebration in Victoria's younger days. H.C. Courtney served as the corps' secretary in 1862, as Victoria readied itself for incorporation as a city.

appointed secretary to the Volunteer Rifle Corps. In 1865 the same paper reported that Courtney, supported by James Bay ward councillor and fellow Irishman Joseph Carey, had been named solicitor for the city. Courtney's offices were at 76 Government Street.

Work was going well and romance was in the air. A young girl by the name of Mary Jane Calder caught his eye. Mary Jane was the daughter of Alexander Calder, an Englishman who had arrived here from England via Kingston, Ontario. The two were married at the Iron Church of St. John in January 1869. By 1871, Courtney had moved his offices to Langley Alley and his wife and family to Pandora Street, but that September, tragedy struck.

Mary Jane and her son were visiting in Moody's Mills (now North Vancouver) on the north shore of Burrard Inlet. While playing on a balcony behind the house they were visiting, the boy fell head first off the balcony into shallow water and was killed. His distraught parents brought his body back to Victoria and buried him in the Quadra Street Burying Ground.

Courtney was devastated by this loss, but threw himself into his work, and his career carried on apace. In 1876, barely 40 years old, he was sworn in as the city's police magistrate. By this time his offices were on Douglas Street. He moved his wife and sons, Knox and Arthur, to a fine home at Cook Street and Rockland Avenue. A daughter, Ethel, was born in 1878. In early 1881, Henry Courtney returned to private practice in the Cariboo, but he died at Soda Creek in November that same year.

After his death, Mary Jane and the children went to live with her father. In 1888, tragedy struck the family yet again. Ten-year-old Ethel was sent home from school complaining of a violent headache. A few days later she was dead, the victim of "brain fever." Mary Jane and the boys moved back to their home at Cook and Rockland. She died there in 1925. Knox became law clerk of the Legislative Assembly and Arthur practised law, so the name of Courtney continued to be associated with legal pursuits in the city.

Courtenay and Courtney—interesting stories both, but which man is the street named after? Well, here's the answer. Captain G.W. Courtenay is remembered in the up-Island town of Courtenay and Courtenay River and—although lamentably misspelled—downtown Victoria's Courtney Street.

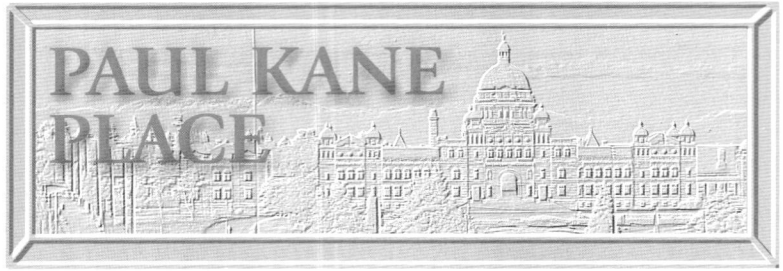

Celebrated artist visited Victoria

Just across the Inner Harbour from the street named for Captain Courtenay, RN, is a short lane in the Songhees development that reminds us of another water-borne wanderer. Paul Kane was an adventurer of a different sort. Courtenay sailed the oceans; Kane followed inland waterways across this continent, creating a fascinating visual and written record as he went.

Because he lived and died in Toronto, many assume, erroneously, that the celebrated artist was Canadian- born, but in his introduction to *Wanderings of an Artist Among the Indians of North America,* Lawrence Burpee tells us that Paul Kane was born in the village of Mallow, Co. Cork, Ireland. His father, Michael, was a native of Preston in Lancashire, England, a corporal in the British army's Royal Horse Artillery. By the time he obtained his discharge in Cork in 1801, he had married Frances Loach and was the father of two. He settled his family in Mallow, where six more children were born.

Paul and Harriet Kane

Paul was the Kanes' sixth child and fourth son. He was nine years old when his father decided to move the family to the pioneer settlement of York (now Toronto) in Upper Canada in about 1819. "Muddy York," as the township was known, was home in the early 1800s to a mixture of white families, Natives, Metis, and French voyageurs. In those pre-Ottawa days, York was the capital of the province. It was situated on the north shore of Lake Ontario, on land sold to the government by the Mississauga Indians.

From the beginning, Kane was fascinated by the Native people who freely roamed the land both inside and outside the confines of the settlement. Like many a young fellow before him, he dreamed of travelling west, where he had heard that buffalo roamed amid lakes, rivers, and snow-capped mountains. He determined to study art so that he could capture the images he found there.

Schooling finished, he found employment as a furniture decorator and sign painter. Later he turned to portrait painting, and by the time he was 26 had made enough money to go to the United States. Wandering from place to place, he was often practically penniless. He found portrait work wherever he could, and on one occasion even painted a steamboat captain's portrait as payment for his fare.

In 1841 he sailed for Europe. Travelling through France and Italy, he visited galleries, marvelled at the work of the great artists, and copied several of their paintings. Four years later he returned to Canada and dedicated himself to painting a series of pictures that would illustrate North American Natives and scenery.

In June 1845, carrying only his portfolio, paints, gun, and ammunition, he travelled north, sketching as he went. This trip was cut short on the advice of a man in Sault Ste Marie, who warned that a solo journey was dangerous and suggested that Kane contact HBC governor Sir George Simpson. Impressed with the artist's sketches and sympathetic to his plight, Simpson commissioned a series of twelve paintings from him and offered free transportation in company canoes. Thus began the most remarkable journey of Paul Kane's life.

He left Toronto in May 1846, headed for Fort Garry (now Winnipeg), Norway House, Fort Edmonton, and Jasper House by canoe, portage, and horse. The inevitable hazards of the journey—appalling weather conditions, accidents, attack by hostile Natives—were tempered by the excitement of a buffalo hunt, the appreciation of the splendour of the countryside, and the opportunity to sketch Native people in their own environment and record their customs and activities in his journal.

In December Kane finally reached Fort Vancouver in Oregon Territory, largest of the HBC strongholds. He was greeted by Chief Factor James Douglas, who had long since given up hope of his arrival. On the West Coast, Kane first encountered Flathead Indians, distinguished by their custom of binding babies' foreheads to press them flat, creating a wedge-shaped skull with a pointed crown.

In March 1847, Kane and some Native companions left Fort Vancouver in a small wooden canoe, bound for Fort Victoria on Vancouver Island. He stopped on the way to sketch Mount St. Helens, avoided by Indians and whites alike because of its tendency to suddenly shoot a long stream of white smoke from its crater. In Victoria, Roderick Finlayson greeted them and gave Kane a comfortable room at the fort for use during his stay.

He spent the next three months sketching on the Island and on the mainland coast. In June 1847 he bade farewell to Finlayson and started the long journey home, travelling by canoe back to Fort Vancouver, then retracing his way east, up the Columbia River, through the Rockies, across the prairies, and back to Ontario. Kane returned from his western sojourn in October 1848 with almost 400 field sketches, many of which he transferred onto canvas.

In 1853 he married Harriet Clench of Toronto, an artist in her own right and loyal supporter of her husband's efforts. They settled in Toronto and raised two daughters and a son. Harriet helped Kane turn his journal scribblings into a book manuscript. *Wanderings of an Artist Among the Indians of North America* was published in London, England, in 1859.

Sadly, by this time Kane's vision had started to fail. For the man whose trained eye and sharp

pencil had so skilfully captured the first images of Indian life across the vastness of Canada, this was the cruellest blow of all. By the mid-1860s he was no longer able to paint. In 1871 he died suddenly and was buried in Toronto's St. James Cemetery, next to the father who had brought him from Ireland more than 50 years before.

Remarkable story. Remarkable man. Once upon a time there was a street named after him in downtown Victoria, but in the early 1900s, when Broughton Street was extended from Douglas Street through to Wharf Street, Kane Street was eliminated. In recent times, during creation of the Songhees development, another street was named after Paul Kane, the man who created the first pictorial record of the first people of Vancouver Island, a century and a half ago.

Some examples of Paul Kane's art: On page 124, clockwise from bottom left, are a self-portrait; Saw-se-a, a Cowichan chief; and a medicine man with mask from Strait of Juan de Fuca, all from 1847. On this page, above, is a sketch of Natives drying salmon on the Dalles, Columbia River, while below is a romanticized depiction of the return of a war party.

The sad story of James Sangster

Memories keep a person alive, at least in the minds of those who follow. But James Sangster had no children. There are no descendants to remember his life, and a dearth of information about his death. Only a short street out in Colwood marks his time in Victoria. Let's see if we can piece together the fabric of his sad and lonely existence.

According to Hudson's Bay Company records, Sangster was born in Port Glasgow, Scotland, around 1808. There is no mention of his father, but his mother's name was Mary. He was one of four children—two boys, two girls.

The family might already have moved to London by the time Sangster, still a teenager, signed on with the HBC's naval department. He was described as a "Boy" on the *Eagle* in September 1827, and he served aboard that ship for five years.

In 1832 Sangster, now classed as "Seaman," transferred to the *Vancouver*. Over the next twenty years he worked aboard the *Cadboro*, *Lama*, *Beaver*, and *Cowlitz*, sailing from London to the HBC's Columbia District and rising through the ranks as he went. He was master of the *Beaver* in 1839 and again in 1843. By 1844 he had become second mate on the *Cowlitz*. In 1847 he took time out to be a clerk in charge of pilotage at Fort Vancouver, then returned to the sea as master of the *Cadboro* and the *Una*.

In 1848 he wrote to James Douglas at Fort Vancouver concerning the demise of his former sailing vessel. The *Vancouver* was, he said, "a total wreck, and we are busy saving all the goods we can, and think tomorrow will be the last day we will get anything from her, as she is breaking up fast." He talked about the need to dry out the goods that had been rescued and asked for advice on what to pay the Indians, "who have been of much assistance in going off to the vessel in canoes ... without their assistance we could not have saved so much as we have done."

In 1851 Sangster retired and moved to Victoria. Over the next years he served as pilot, harbour master, collector of customs, and Victoria's first postmaster. In his *Reminiscences*, Dr. John Helmcken remembers Sangster well and describes how he sat up on Beacon Hill, spyglass in hand, watching for Company ships or other expected vessels to round Rocky Point.

When he was postmaster, according to Helmcken, Sangster occupied the log house at Fort Victoria that was "on the right as you entered by the front [Wharf Street] gate." He seems not to have been much of a "people person," preferring to hand letters out through

Two years after the HBC's SS Beaver *arrived on the West Coast, James Sangster served as its captain. The* Beaver, *a 101-foot vessel made of British oak, fir, and African teak, was the first steam paddlewheeler to ply the waters of the North Pacific. In 1843, James Douglas and his working party sailed into the harbour aboard the* Beaver, *ready to build Fort Victoria.*

a specially installed window so that people did not have to go into the house.

Helmcken describes Sangster as "an exceedingly good-hearted, quiet, unobtrusive man, whom all liked," but added that he "liked whiskey also" and was "often shaky after drinking." This may have been why he so carefully guarded his privacy. And it may have played a part in his decision, in the summer of 1858, to give up his postmaster's job.

By this time, Victoria's gold rush fever had been burning for more than three months. The first boatload of gold miners arrived from California at the end of April. Hundreds more hurried to Victoria for licences and gold-digging gear. It was an exciting time. But Sangster, no longer able to perform his duties, had elected to retire and, according to the *Victoria Gazette*, bought a farm out in what we now call Colwood. His land stretched from where the gravel pit is today, over to Lagoon Road, an area later known as Sangster Plains.

Somewhere along the way—or maybe it was always thus—Sangster lost touch with his mother in London, England. We learn much about his family dynamics through a remarkable collection of correspondence housed in the HBC Archives. These letters, sent out to company employees on ships, were for some reason not delivered and eventually were

This photo of the interior of Fort Victoria was taken from just inside the fort's Wharf Street gate, close to the log house where postmaster James Sangster handed out the mail. The path through the fort (now Fort Street) passed near the bell tower (centre left), exited the fort's east gate (marked in the sidewalk at Government Street), and continued east through forest, swamp, and meadowlands toward Cadboro Bay.

returned to London, where they lay unopened for several decades.

In one letter, written in June 1840, Sangster's mother chastises him for not keeping in touch or sending her money. She says she has not heard from him in nine years and reminds him: "It is your duty to look to your mother in her old age. I am now 60 and am unable to do needlework as [I] used to do and how can I live on ten pounds a year which you know is all I have." Eventually Mary Sangster writes directly to the HBC for financial aid. She writes repeatedly until she is informed, in reply to her letter of September 11, 1855, that her son has withdrawn the entire account.

Three years later, on October 18, 1858, Sangster committed suicide. His obituary mentions the positions he held, but reveals nothing about his sad life and lonely death. We will probably never know what demons plagued him, what depths of despair drove him to kill himself in his lonely cabin on that bleak October day.

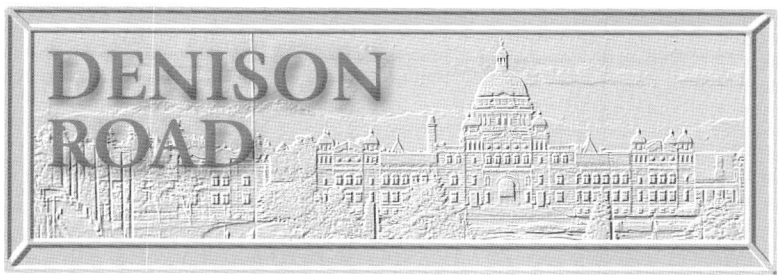

A dedicated weather man

The observatory atop Gonzales Hill is at the end of a steeply curving road that commemorates a dedicated meteorologist. The man for whom Denison Road is named designed that observatory and even lived there for a while. But where did he come from, and what brought him to that windswept point on the south Vancouver Island coastline?

F. (for Francis) Napier Denison was born in 1866 in Toronto, the son of Lieutenant-Colonel Robert B. Denison, who played an important role in the formation of the Upper Canada government. Interested in engineering of an electrical rather than a political sort, eighteen-year-old Napier graduated from Upper Canada College and was appointed assistant observer at the Toronto Observatory. Two years of study at Boston and Lynn, Massachusetts, led him back to Toronto and eventually, in 1898, to a new position on the southern tip of Vancouver Island.

In Victoria, Denison was observer and weather forecaster under E. Baynes Reed. The weather observing station where they worked had been first established at the Esquimalt naval base in 1876 and then moved to several different locations. Just prior to Denison's arrival it relocated to the old post office building on Government Street, north of the new causeway that had recently replaced the old wooden bridge that once crossed James Bay.

At the Government Street premises, Reed and Denison worked together to reach their goal, and on November 1, 1898, the *Daily Colonist* published the first daily weather forecast. In the spring of 1899, they began issuing marine warnings and ensured that storm signals were displayed at sites chosen so they could be seen by ships at sea. As wireless telegraphy advanced, the marine forecasts were broadcast to ships on the Pacific, and observations by ship crews were collated for use in weather analysis.

Francis Napier Denison

Soon it was clear that the weather office was outgrowing its Government Street site. Denison played a large part in the design and development of the new weather station, which was to be built on Gonzales Hill. There were no roads to the top

In the early 1900s, Gonzales Hill was a favourite spot for whiling away a summer's day. With no houses to spoil their view, these children gazed west toward Ross Bay, Clover Point, the outer harbour, and in the distance, the Sooke Hills. The Gonzales Weather Station, built in 1914 on top of Gonzales Hill, was automated in 1964 and still provides weather information to Environment Canada.

in those days. Building materials and supplies were brought around the coastline to Gonzales Bay and hoisted up the 68-metre hill.

By the end of 1914, the Pacific Coast headquarters for the Dominion Meteorological Service was in operation. It recorded weather, star sightings, and seismic readings and was rated the best weather office outside Toronto. The reinforced concrete building, its distinctive dome housing a 12.7-centimetre telescope, could be seen from just about anywhere in Victoria.

When E. Baynes Reed died in 1916, Denison was appointed director of the facility. He provided special summaries and weather forecasts for shipping within a 5,000-kilometre range, advanced his theories of seven-year weather cycles and the effect of sun spots on weather, and gathered evidence to support his belief that the cyclical occurrence of earthquakes coincided with stresses produced by the earth tilting on its axis. His research on weather cycles and seismic occurrences brought him international recognition, and he published several scientific papers and articles.

For navigators using this busy and important West Coast harbour, time was of the essence. Denison bought a small telescope and learned, by star observation, to estimate time accurately to within one-tenth of a second per day. He also operated a seismograph, which measured

Denison Road

This view from the Parliament Buildings, taken during the "Big Snow" of 1916, two years after Denison established the Gonzales Observatory, shows the Empress Hotel at right and the old post office at left (the causeway garage—now the Visitor Information Centre —was erected later). Left of centre is the Belmont Building, on the corner of Humboldt Street, where a rooftop shed housed the mechanism for a time-ball that enabled mariners to rate their chronometers without leaving their vessels.

tremors in the earth's crust. This work eventually proved invaluable for coal-mining operations all over the world, where seismographic readings could be used to predict collapse in a mine and help avert disaster.

With its panoramic views of Victoria, the Strait of Juan de Fuca, and the Sooke Hills, the observatory was the ideal place to work ... and to live. Denison had married Ethel Margaret, daughter of Captain John Walbran, the master mariner who was by that time writing his book on the history and origin of British Columbia coast names. The Denisons, who had no children, resided for a while in James Bay, just a few blocks from the Walbran family residence at the corner of Dallas and Menzies. But so engrossed did Denison become in his activities that he and Ethel moved from their Superior Street home into the observatory, occupying its simple accommodations for more than 20 years.

A confirmed workaholic before anyone coined the term, Denison did not take a statutory holiday in over twenty years. Poor health started him on the road to a well-earned

The white dome of the Dominion Meteorological Service station on top of Gonzales Hill was, and still is, a prominent Victoria landmark. It served as both office and home for Director Denison and his wife over more than two decades.

Each day at 12:55 p.m., the time-ball was raised to the top of the mast. At precisely 1 p.m., an electrical impulse sent through the land-telegraph line from the Gonzales Observatory tripped the mechanism that allowed the time-ball to drop. This system was discontinued around 1930, but the shed that houses the mechanism can be seen on the Belmont Building roof to this day.

retirement in 1933, but he worked another three years so he could receive full pension. Official retirement in 1936 didn't stop his ever-active brain. Always tinkering with new gadgets, he invented a novel form of fire escape and a cabinet dust remover for hospital use.

Ethel died in 1945. A year later her husband was also gone. He died in his Burdett Avenue home at the age of 79 and was buried beside his wife at Royal Oak Cemetery.

Today, Denison Road is the quiet route to one of the most spectacular views in the city.

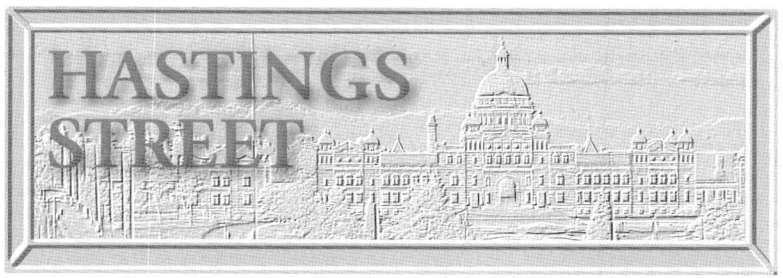

HASTINGS STREET

Stargazer built conservatory

The telescope that Napier Denison used in the observatory atop Gonzales Hill once belonged to Victoria's first astronomer—a fellow with the remarkable name of Oregon Columbus Hastings.

Hastings hailed from Hancock County, Illinois. He was born there in 1846, and a year later followed the Oregon Trail when his father led the family across the plains to Portland. In 1852 they moved to Port Townsend, and one day Hastings Sr. took his son on a schooner voyage across the strait to Vancouver Island.

They sailed into a harbour dominated on its eastern shore by Fort Victoria. Outside the stockade were a few shops, stores, and residences, including the simple house just north of the fort where Governor Richard Blanshard had lived until his return to England the year before.

A handful of trails led off in all directions. One followed the waterfront south, tracing the outline of James Bay until it reached the grand home of Blanshard's successor, Governor James Douglas. One ran east from the fort, through the forest, frog-swamps, and fertile pastures to Cadboro Bay. Others led to the recently established company farms at Esquimalt and beyond. With the settlement's population fast approaching 200, colonial surveyor J.D. Pemberton was hard at work preparing the first town plan. Standing on the deck of his father's schooner, the six-year-old boy from Port Townsend thought it was a very fine place indeed.

When he finished school, the younger Hastings worked on his father's farm for several years. By the age of 28 he was ready to move on and decided to make his home in the place across the water that he had liked so well all those years before. The Victoria that awaited him was greatly changed. In 1874 it was a busy city with a bustling downtown. There was even talk of a grand new city hall on the street named after Sir James Douglas, now retired and living quietly in his James Bay mansion.

O.C. Hastings

Hastings, who had studied photography as a pastime, found a job as manager of Spencer's photographic business on Fort Street. In May 1867 he married Matilda

Birch, originally from Dungeness in Scotland. She died in 1881. Three years later Hastings married again, this time to a woman with a name almost as exotic as his own.

Silvestria Theodora Layzell Smith, an Australian by birth, had arrived in Victoria with her family in 1858 and at the age of sixteen had married mining businessman Philip Smith. In the 1860s Smith owned a pack train, hotel, bakery, and blacksmith shop in the Cariboo. The gold rush was in full swing. He was hugely successful. Then a road was blasted through the Fraser Canyon and traffic was diverted through Yale. Smith's business in Port Douglas went belly-up. He went to California to recoup his fortunes and died there in 1871, leaving a wife, three sons, and a daughter in Victoria to mourn him.

By the time she met O.C. Hastings, Silvestria Smith had had more than her fair share of challenges ... and invented a few of her own. A single parent in those days had precious little support or clout in the community, and Silvestria vowed to give women a voice. One cold January morning in 1875, when the town turned out to vote for a new mayor, Silvestria took her place in the pages of Victoria's history by becoming the first woman to cast a vote.

The men of the town were aghast. O.C. Hastings was delighted. This high-spirited creature was a woman after his own heart. In 1884 the two were married.

Hastings was now the proud owner of the Fort Street photography business, which boasted patrons far and wide. The family's first home, on Elizabeth Street between Cook and Chambers above Pandora, was eventually too small for the growing brood—O.C. and Silvestria had had a young daughter of their own—and they moved, first to Chatham Street, then to a fine home up

Silvestria Hastings is pictured with the children—John, Philip, Alfred, and Elizabeth —from her first marriage. Silvestria and O.C. also had a daughter of their own.

the Fort Street hill. It was here, in 1891, that Hastings built a house on the east side of St. Charles Street, about halfway between Cadboro Bay Road (as that part of Fort Street was then called) and Belcher Street (later renamed Rockland Avenue). And it was here that he indulged a long-time passion—astronomy. He built an observatory on top of the rocks in his own backyard and equipped it with an expensive telescope. He became a member of the British Astronomical Association. Amateur astronomers from far and wide visited "Observatory Hill" to study the stars and planets.

Around the turn of the century, Hastings' fortunes changed. He sold the St. Charles Street

Astronomers from far and wide visited the observatory O.C. Hastings built behind his St. Charles Street home, on what was called Observatory Hill.

property and moved his family to 727 Herald Street. Predeceasing Silvestria by more than a decade, Hastings died after a short illness in August 1912 ... just about the same time a fellow by the name of Denison was drawing up plans for Victoria's new weather station. Two years later, Hastings' precious telescope had found a new home.

His private viewing station is gone, but in Saanich, a road that runs between Interurban and Granville reminds us of the remarkable man with the unusual name who once lived on "Observatory Hill."

HARRISON STREET

Adventures filled route to Victoria

A few blocks north of Hastings' observatory, Harrison Street gives no hint of who it's named for. However, a hundred years ago one of its Fort Street corners boasted an impressive home built for an equally impressive local personage—Judge Eli Harrison Jr. The Harrisons had been in Victoria since 1858, when Eli's father, Eli Harrison Sr. brought his family up the coast from California. But our story begins a long time before that, when the adventurous Harrison boys left England, bound for the New World.

The Harrisons hailed from the County of Cheshire. Eli, the oldest brother, was born there in 1824. On leaving school he journeyed to India and then to Rome, where he became skilled in the art of church mural painting. Eventually he returned to England and in 1847 married fifteen-year-old Elizabeth Warburton in Liverpool. Three years later the young couple and Eli's brothers George, William, and John were on their way to America to rejoin their father, Samuel, who, following up his American family connections, had bought land in Arkansas and travelled ahead.

Elizabeth was only fifteen years old when she married Eli Harrison Sr.

The younger Harrisons landed on the east coast, but never did find their father. They assumed he must have been killed or drowned as he made his way up the Mississippi. The brothers moved through Georgia and on to New Orleans. Talk of West Coast gold was tempting, and soon they were on their way across country with a Mormon caravan on its way to Salt Lake City. The Mormons were impressed by Eli's painting prowess, but puzzled by his puritanical attitude toward marriage.

After a while the philosophical rifts became too wide, and the Harrisons moved west once more, into the setting sun. This time they were self-sufficient. Not for them the long wagon trains that carried several family groups for safety. The Harrison party crossed the vast plains alone in two "prairie schooners," Elizabeth holding her Missouri-born son firmly on her lap.

It was a journey fraught with danger and challenges that none of them could have anticipated. Decades later, one tale would be recounted many times without ever losing its dramatic impact. This was the story of the encounter with a Sioux chieftain who tried to persuade the young parents that their fair-haired, light-eyed boy would make a wonderful leader for his tribe. The Harrisons couldn't know that many miles away, on an island they had yet to see, a Scottish mother by the name of Joan Dunsmuir had recently braved a similar experience, when a group of Kwakiutl women "borrowed" her blond, blue-eyed son James with the idea of making him their leader.

Eventually the little party reached California. John, who started studying to be a doctor, died in Almadore County. His brothers mined gold. The gold rush was almost over, but new finds to the north were making news. The Harrisons purchased tickets on a steamship bound for Victoria and hastened to check them out.

After the harrowing trip across America, the rough sea voyage from San Francisco was the last straw for Elizabeth. No matter what awaited her on Vancouver Island, it couldn't be as bad as what had gone before. When the *Brother Jonathan* sailed into Esquimalt, Elizabeth put her foot down. No more travelling. So the family settled here, and it's fortunate for us that they did, or we might never have been privileged to hear about their many exploits.

Eli Jr. and Agnes, children of Eli Sr. and Elizabeth.

Eli Jr. attended school in Victoria, then studied law. He prepared for the bar under the direction of eminent lawyer George W. Pearkes until the latter's untimely death. In 1871 he applied successfully to the Supreme Court for admittance as attorney and solicitor, along with a young man by the name of Theodore Davie, who would later become premier of B.C. By 1875 Eli Jr. was called to the bar, and in 1878 was made clerk of the House of Assembly.

In 1880 Eli, now assistant attorney-general, married Eunice Seabrook, who had arrived here with her family from London, Ontario, in 1864. Eunice's father, Roads Seabrook, was a prominent local businessman, soon to be vice-president of R.P. Rithet & Co. Ltd. The two were married at St. John's Church. Eunice's most valued wedding gift was a silk opera bag from a friend of her grandmother—Queen Victoria.

The Harrisons lived in a cottage on Birdcage Walk, near Eli's government office, before moving with their growing family of six to a fine new home at 1323 Harrison Street, up on the Fort Street hill. The senior Harrisons lived close by. Like his father before him, Eli Jr. had become an enthusiastic Freemason. He was Grand Master in 1878, 1880, and 1881, and during his first term he consecrated the Masonic Temple at the corner of Douglas and Fisgard streets, near Victoria's brand-new red-brick city hall.

In his capacity as crown prosecutor for the Cariboo, Eli Jr. travelled extensively through B.C.'s Interior. His many adventures, recorded by Eunice and including notes he wrote himself, were published in the *Northwest Digest* after Eunice's death.

By 1907 Eli Sr. had died. Elizabeth lived until 1926. Eli Jr. died in 1930, and Eunice followed him twenty years later. They are gone but far from forgotten. The many descendants of this remarkable family—and the street that bears its name—remind us of them to this day.

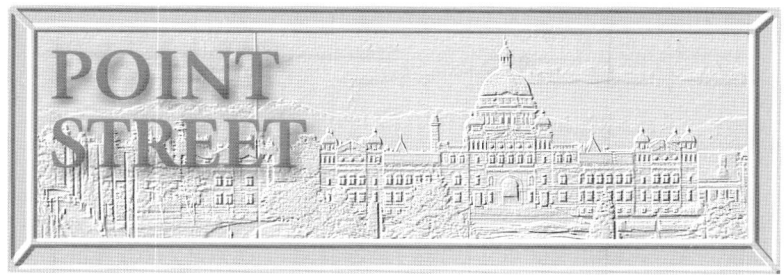

There's a story to that Point

We seem to have lots of Spits and Heads and Arms around Victoria, all named after somebody and all of consuming interest. But for now we're pointing the finger at a few points around the local coastline. Who or what are they named after?

Some, like Rocky Point or Thumb Point, seem obvious (look at the latter's shape on the map!); others are more obscure. Some are tied to street names; others remind us of people we knew, or visitors from another time and place.

Billings Point (Sooke Basin) recalls William Thomas Billings, a Royal Navy surgeon who served under Captain Kellett on the surveying vessel *Herald,* here with the *Pandora* in 1846.

Cattle Point (Oak Bay) was where livestock, brought across the water from the mainland, were pushed overboard in the rocky bay, rounded up, and herded along the rough waterfront trail (now Beach Drive) to the slaughterhouse on the site of today's Royal Victoria Yacht Club.

Christie Point (Portage Inlet) was named after John Christie, who in the mid-1930s became the owner of the long peninsula that juts into Portage Inlet and was once part of Craigflower Farm.

Cormorant Point (Gordon Head) is not named after the birds that often skim the surface of the seas but after Her Majesty's paddle-sloop *Cormorant*, the first naval steam vessel in these waters. The ship's captain, Commander G.T. Gordon, named the point.

Ellice Point (Victoria Harbour) was named by officers of the Hudson's Bay Company after the Right Honourable Edward Ellice, conservative MP for Coventry, England, who joined the fur trade in 1803 and was HBC deputy-governor by the time he died in 1863.

Finlayson Point, off Dallas Road on the south side of Beacon Hill Park, is named after Roderick Finlayson, the Scottish-born HBC man who was in charge of Fort Victoria from 1844, chief factor in 1859, and mayor of Victoria in 1878.

Harling Point, once called Chinese Point, was named for Dr. Fred Harling, a dentist who lived in the area in the 1930s and died tragically after attempting to rescue the occupants of a small boat that had overturned in stormy seas at Foul Bay.

Helgesen Point (Pedder Bay) takes its name from the Helgesen family. Hans Helgesen, originally from Norway, came to B.C. in 1858 to look for gold. In 1862 he married an Irish girl he had met in San Francisco and they settled

Point No Point, pictured in the 1940s, gained its unusual name from the fact that it was seen either as a point, or not as a point, depending on which direction you were looking along the coastline.

Looking across the harbour toward the Sooke Hills, this 1860 Edmund T. Coleman painting shows the first James Bay Bridge and, beyond it, a heavily treed Laurel Point.

Point Street

Macaulay Point was originally part of Donald Macaulay's Viewfield Farm. It looks little changed from when Richard Maynard took this photo in 1878.

in Metchosin, where their descendants live to this day.

Macaulay Point formed the southernmost tip of Donald Macaulay's Viewfield Farm at Esquimalt in 1850. After ten years, Macaulay had only managed to clear 35 of his 600 rocky acres. He gave up the farm and took charge of the powder magazine at Esquimalt. In 1868 he drowned in Esquimalt Harbour when a munitions barge sprung a leak.

McLoughlin Point (part of the DND property) reminds us of Dr. John McLoughlin, head of the HBC's Columbia Department based at Fort Vancouver on the Columbia River. In 1842 it was his assistant, James Douglas, who chose the place we now call Victoria to be the site of the company's new northern headquarters.

McMicking Point, at the southwest corner of the Victoria Golf Course, is named for Ontario-born entrepreneur Robert Burns McMicking, who brought electric street lights to the downtown core and later installed the province's first telephone system in a building in Trounce Alley.

Moses Point, at the north end of Deep Cove, once belonged to Daniel David Moses, a Welshman who came to Saanich via San Francisco and the Cariboo. Moses ran a hotel in Victoria, while his wife managed the hop farm on their North Saanich property.

Ogden Point, at the entrance to Victoria Harbour, commemorates Montrealer Peter Skene Ogden, who joined the North West Company in 1811 and rose through the ranks to become one of the HBC's top men on the West Coast. The Ogden Point Docks were completed during the First World War.

Saxe Point in Esquimalt recalls Queen Victoria's beloved husband, HRH Prince Albert of Saxe-Coburg and Gotha, who died at Windsor Castle of typhoid fever at the age of 42 in 1861. Elements of his name are evident along that part of the coastline that follows Royal Roads from Victoria Harbour to Albert Head.

Sheringham Point, pictured in the 1920s, was named after Commander William Louis Sheringham, RN, a surveying officer who served in the Navy from 1808 until his death in 1873.

Saxe Point is named after Queen Victoria's beloved husband. She never recovered from his early demise, wearing black till the day she died on the Isle of Wight, England, in 1901.

Point Street

Foul (Gonzales) Bay in the foreground was so named because the many rocks under the surface of its sheltered waters inspired early sailors to describe it as a "foul anchorage." The long, thin strip of Clover Point, once covered with knee-high red clover, can be seen in the distance.

Sheringham Point, west of Sooke, was named in 1790 after Commander William Louis Sheringham, who entered the service as a surveying officer in 1808, was made captain in 1847, and vice-admiral in 1871. He died in 1873.

Yarrows Point, at Coles Bay, reminds us of Sir Alfred Yarrow, who in 1914 purchased a shipyard at Esquimalt. His son Norman retired 32 years later, having successfully expanded the family's business to North Vancouver.

And last but not least, there's the strange-sounding **Point No Point**, so called when geographic survey teams decided that whether the point existed or not depended on which way you happened to be facing. Looking out across Juan de Fuca Strait from Jordan River, the coastline to the south clearly jutted out in a point. But looking north from the direction of Sooke, the point wasn't visible. So from one direction, there was a **Point**, but from the other direction there was ... **No Point**.

By the way, Clover Street and Point Street are just north of Dallas Road near, you guessed it, **Clover Point**. In the early 1850s the weed known as Scotch broom—introduced by a homesick Scottish settler—strangled much of the natural plant life in this area. Only its name reminds us that knee-high red clover once grew along the waterfront at Clover Point.

Interesting, isn't it? And now next time someone asks, "What's the Point?" you'll know exactly what to say!

This 1885 view of the Inner Harbour shows Laurel Point (centre), and in the distance, McLoughlin and Work Points.

Looking over Michael Finnerty's land in the early 1890s, Ten Mile Point (named for its nautical distance from Esquimalt Harbour) can be seen in the distance.

Medana's farm was James Bay picnic site

Not far from Dallas Road's Holland Point was the home of early James Bay farmer Paul Medana.

Not much is known about Medana—or Medina, as he was sometimes later called—but we do know that he was born in Italy in 1813. He arrived in Victoria during the heady gold-rush era of the late 1850s with money in his pocket, which he shrewdly invested in real estate. In January 1859, the *Gazette* announced that property at Yates and Government streets, leased from Dr. George Johnston by Medana and two others, was now available for re-lease.

At that time, little was left of Fort Victoria in the area bounded by Wharf, Broughton, Government, and Bastion streets. The settlement—not yet a town—was rapidly spreading north and west to accommodate newcomers. On its southern border, James Bay was a real bay—a shallow inlet extending east from the harbour almost to where the Church of Our Lord now stands on the corner of Blanshard and Belleville.

The bay was spanned by a wooden bridge that stretched from the south end of Government Street to a point just north and west of Governor James Douglas's residence. West of the bridge, on a grassy slope facing the

The only known photograph of a solemn Paul Medana (standing, left) in full Masonic garb, with J. Ragazzoni and an unidentified fellow Mason.

harbour, stood Victoria's first, pagoda-like Parliament Buildings.

Behind those buildings, much of the rest of the peninsula that we now call James Bay

At the bottom centre of this 1889 bird's eye view of Victoria is the southern portion of the James Bay peninsula, which was the location of Medina's Grove.

belonged to the Hudson's Bay Company. In the mid-1850s, former employee William Sims leased a large portion of it from the HBC for 50 cents an acre. He named it Bexley Farm, after his new wife's birthplace in England, but the same careless corruption that would later change Medana to Medina changed Bexley to Beckley.

Paul Medana was the second man to farm on the James Bay peninsula. He chose a huge tract of land on the south side, facing the Strait of Juan de Fuca, and built a fine home for his wife Mary and their large family near the corner of Menzies Street and Dallas Road. Built on solid stone, the house had nine rooms. There were outbuildings and stables for horses, dogs, and other animals, and a boathouse near the waterfront, opposite the majestic mountains of the Olympic Peninsula.

Mary Helen Medana

Medana Street

In 1855, the remains of people buried on the south side of the ravine north of Fort Victoria (now Johnson Street) were taken by prison chain-gangs up to Victoria's first officially designated cemetery—the Old Burying Ground on Quadra Street. Paul Medana was one of 1,000 people buried there up to 1872, at which point the cemetery was full. Ross Bay Cemetery opened in 1873. The Quadra Street Burying Ground was turned into a public park—Pioneer Square—by the city in the early 1900s.

Medana seemed more interested in real estate investment than in farming, and much of his land remained undeveloped. Medina's Grove, as it was mistakenly called, stretched from Simcoe Street south to Dallas Road, and from Menzies Street west to Pilot Street. It was a wonderful, wild place, covered with massive oak trees and shrubs, containing clearings of various sizes that were ideal for picnics. There were no fences, and the area soon became a firm favourite with local residents. Most people approached the Grove from the corner of Menzies and Simcoe, quickly losing themselves in the splendour of the tall trees, meadows, and wildflower-strewn slopes leading to the sparkling waters of the strait.

In mid-1868, a decade after his arrival, Medana fell ill, and in November of that year he suffered an aneurysm and died. His fellow Freemasons gathered at the Masonic Hall on Fisgard Street before proceeding to James Bay. With due ceremony, and preceded by the Volunteer Band, the coffin was carried up the Quadra Street hill to the burying ground that since 1855 had provided a final resting place for many of Victoria's early pioneers.

Four years after Medana's death, his James Bay property became the focus of debate. With the Quadra Street cemetery now full to overflowing, the city was looking for a new place to bury its dead. Where better, thought the cemetery board trustees, than part of Paul

Medana's beautiful acreage overlooking the Strait of Juan de Fuca?

James Bay residents, horrified at the thought of losing their favourite pleasure ground, objected strongly. There was no point in sacrificing a perfectly good picnic place for a cemetery, they said. It too would be full soon enough, and then the search for yet another cemetery would begin, but by that time, Medana's Grove as they knew it would be gone for good.

The city turned its attentions elsewhere. In 1873 Ross Bay Cemetery was officially opened, and Medana's Grove was granted a reprieve. But in 1880 it was subdivided. Trees were felled, land was cleared, streets were created. One street running from Niagara to Dallas was called Medina, but was later renamed Boyd Street after the purchaser of those lots.

It's good to know that the man the *Colonist* described as "an amicable, upright and generous-hearted citizen" is gone but not forgotten. In Pioneer Square a tall monument, angled with age but remarkably well preserved, bears the words "In Memory Of Paul Medana, Native of Italy, Died November 14, 1868, aged 53 years." And at the eastern edge of what once was James Bay's favourite picnic area, a quiet, tree-lined street bears Paul Medana's name.

EARLE STREET

Adding a little spice to life

Thomas Earle would feel quite at home on lower Yates Street today, where the smell of freshly ground coffee can bring a smile to the sourest early-morning face. In his day, the aroma was even more pungent. For this was where the citizens of Victoria came to purchase fine imported teas, coffees, and spices from the store that still stands where he left it 90 years ago. Groceries were far from Earle's mind when he first arrived in Victoria in 1865, however. He had come, like so many others, to dig for Cariboo gold.

Earle was born in Lansdowne Township, Leeds County, Ontario, in 1837, the son of an Irishman who had settled in Western Ontario in the early 1800s. Earle first ventured into business as the operator of a general store in Brockville, but in his early twenties he packed his belongings and headed west. The long journey brought him to the fast-growing town of Victoria in 1862. Earle was destined to make money there, but in those early days he was much more interested in mining for gold.

Thomas and Lizzie Earle

In the Cariboo, success eluded him. Two years in Williams Creek were enough to convince him that his fortunes lay elsewhere after all, and he returned to the Island. Since its incorporation as a city in 1862, Victoria had continued to grow. Earle had no difficulty finding employment as bookkeeper for J. Rueffe's grocery business. Rumours of gold finds continued to tantalize him, and in 1867 he travelled north to Big Bend, where he catered to the miners with a general store on French Creek. This time he was successful, returning with enough money to buy a share in his former employer's grocery. When Rueffe died in 1873, Earle bought out his interest and ran the business himself.

In January 1875, Earle married Lizzie, the

The Thomas Earle residence at 131 Cadboro Bay Road (later renumbered 1461 Fort Street) was surrounded by gardens where the parents could relax and the children could play safely, away from the busy road.

daughter of Victoria resident Jesse Mason. Eventually they moved into a new house on Cadboro Bay Road, as the narrow part of Fort Street was then called. It was a comfortable, cottage-style house set back from the road on the south side between Pemberton and St. Charles. In the days before electric streetcars rattled up the Fort Street hill, the rambling home with its large covered front porch and spacious gardens was a quiet, pleasant place for Thomas, Lizzie, and their five children.

Business was booming. By 1881, Earle's Victoria Coffee and Spice Mills were firmly ensconced in a building next to the Occidental Hotel on Wharf Street, at the foot of Johnson. Here there was plenty of room for his wholesale groceries and space on the first floor for a spice-canning department.

By now Earle was also engaged in other activities. He became involved with railroad construction on the Island and in Oregon and Washington, and had an interest in a number of quartz mines in the Selkirk Mountains. Soon he was immersed in municipal politics. Elected to municipal council in 1885, he was urged to stand for mayor but refused. Eventually he gave way to pressure and entered into "politics proper," joining forces with fellow staunch

Earle Street

Architect Thomas Hooper designed Earle's business establishment near the Occidental Hotel, which is pictured here in 1860 at the corner of Johnson and Wharf streets.

Conservative E.G. Prior, who owned a thriving hardware business just up Johnson Street at the corner of Government. In 1891 Victorians elected them to the House of Commons. It was an unbeatable combination. In 1896 and 1900 they were elected again.

Meanwhile, Earle's coffee and spice business was doing well and it became clear the Wharf Street warehouse was no longer adequate. By the turn of the century, Earle was the proud occupant of a brand-new Thomas Hooper-designed building around the corner. The *Colonist* was impressed. In 1901 it declared, "Among the last year's most pretentious additions to the business houses of the city, none is more modern and substantial than the new premises erected on lower Yates Street by Mr. Thomas Earle."

Indeed it was a fine-looking edifice with an impressive facade that, 100 years later, is as eye-catching as the day it was built. Small turrets adorned the two upper front corners. Large windows allowed in the maximum possible amount of light. All four floors were piled high with stock, carried by an electric elevator from the main floor. A track ran from the elevator out to the sidewalk, where a big-wheeled covered cart bearing the words "Thos. Earle, Wholesale Grocer" stood ready at the curb.

This 1864 view south from the Occidental Hotel along the waterfront, past the Fort Victoria site and over toward Laurel Point (at centre), is the same view that would have greeted Thomas Earle when he arrived in Victoria one year later.

The business should have made Earle a rich man, but unfortunately he began to neglect it in favour of his political activities. Eventually the business failed and he retired. A lifetime of hard work was over. Broken and discouraged, he died at the age of 73 at his home up on the Fort Street hill.

The building in which he prospered still stands at 530 Yates Street as a monument to his better days. And not far south of where his family home once stood, a short street in Fairfield reminds us of the man who added spice to the lives of Victorians in days gone by.

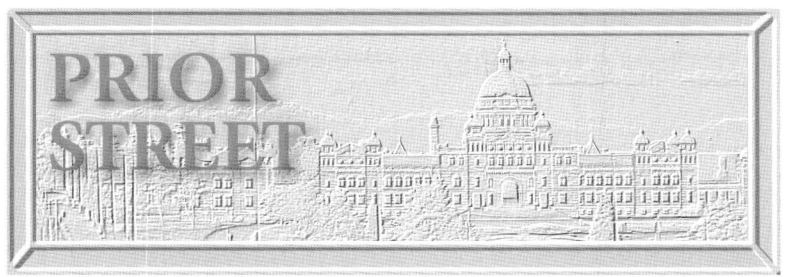

Practical, pragmatic politician

Up around Hillside, street names are a family affair. John Work's huge Hillside Farm covered the area from Hillside Avenue to Bay Street and from Quadra to Cook. Today, streets within these boundaries remind us of Work's wife, sons, and sons-in-law. One of the latter occupied B.C.'s two highest offices. His name was Edward Gawler Prior.

Prior, the son of an English clergyman, was born near Ripon, Yorkshire, in 1853. Twenty years later, with his mining engineer papers in his pocket, he set sail on the *Adriatic* from Liverpool, bound for Victoria and a job with the Vancouver Coal Mining and Land Company. His ability to work well with the miners led to his appointment, in 1878, as B.C.'s first Inspector of Mines and an opportunity to practise the skills that would later serve him well in his political career.

In 1878, six years after his arrival in Victoria, Prior married Suzette, youngest of John and Josette Work's eight daughters. Two of Suzette's older sisters had also married well-known local personages—Sarah was Mrs. Roderick Finlayson and Jane was Mrs. W.F. Tolmie—who were contemporaries of her father. But by this time, John Work was dead. It was Suzette's brother David who walked her down the aisle of the old iron church of St. John, on the corner of Douglas and Fisgard streets.

After their marriage, the Priors lived on Fort Street until they moved to Nanaimo. They returned to Victoria in 1880 and lived on Burdett Street. In the early 1880s, Prior bought four acres of land just a few blocks south of Suzette's family home. He was moving up in social and political circles. He wanted a larger house for his wife and three children, and more importantly, a home that would be suitable for entertaining on a grand scale.

Architect John Teague's design was brought to life by John Hill, who used only the finest building materials. The seven imported fireplaces were backed and faced with steel. Elegant mantels were complemented

Lieut.-Col. E.G. Prior cut a fine figure in his 5th Regiment regalia.

E.G. Prior's fine home at 620 St. Charles Street, built in 1913, was the second major Prior residence in the Rockland area. Prior lived here with his second wife Genevieve and their family.

by black walnut doors with unique brass door handles, gleaming in the light from tall windows that reached up to high ceilings. A magnificent staircase led to the second floor, which contained six sleeping apartments, a nursery, and a bathroom. Hot and cold running water was a feature in every room, along with electric bells and every modern convenience.

By January 1885 the 6,000-square-foot "Stoneyhurst," as the Priors first thought to call it, was ready for occupancy. With an imposing front entrance at the top of a winding path from Rockland Avenue (later relocated onto Pemberton Street), the house was surrounded by woods and gardens and had a wonderful view south over the ocean. The name was soon changed to "The Priory," and hardly a week went by without mention of some social event or other at this beautifully appointed residence.

The 1880s were exciting years for Prior. He had come a long way from his beginnings as a mining engineer. In 1874, while still in Nanaimo, he had indulged his fondness for the military by joining a rifle company. Six years later he was colonel in command of the 5th Regiment Garrison Artillery, based in Victoria.

In 1880, when it became clear that his government position offered little opportunity for advancement, Prior resigned and bought into a Yates Street hardware business owned and operated successfully in Victoria by Alfred Fellows since 1859. With a winning combination of energy, enthusiasm, and enterprise, Prior helped build the store into a

Prior Street

The Prior Block has been much altered over the years, but stands on the northeast corner of Government and Johnson streets to this day.

firm worthy of incorporation in 1891. Newly located at Government and Johnson streets, E.G. Prior & Co. had branches in Vancouver and Kamloops and conducted business through offices in London and New York.

He was elected a member of the provincial legislature in 1886, serving till 1888, when he resigned in order to seek the federal seat vacated by Noah Shakespeare, who had recently been appointed Victoria's postmaster. Prior was returned by acclamation and was re-elected three times in the next twelve years.

During this time, he was widowed. Suzette died in 1897 after a lengthy illness, leaving her husband with a son and three daughters. Two years later, Prior married Victoria-born Genevieve Wright. They built a home on the west side of St. Charles Street, a stone's throw away from the magnificent mansion that would become his finest—and final—home.

Fhe 5th Regiment performing a sham battle in Beacon Hill Park in honour of Queen Victoria's Diamond Jubilee, ca 1897.

By 1916, when this photo was taken, Prior's store stood on one of the busiest intersections in town.

In 1902, Prior returned to provincial politics. He served as minister of mines, then succeeded James Dunsmuir as premier of B.C. Barely six months into his term of office, Prior was asked to resign when a government contract awarded to his firm was deemed to present a conflict of interest. He returned to his favourite pastimes—theatre, tennis, and local affairs—but couldn't stay away from politics. By 1919 he was lieutenant-governor of B.C. Now he and Genevieve were residents of Government House, a relatively painless move from their St. Charles Street home.

This was the pinnacle of Prior's career. Unfortunately he enjoyed it for less than twelve months. He was taken ill while attending a tennis exhibition and died a month later at Royal Jubilee Hospital. A state funeral marked his passing and he was laid to rest in Ross Bay Cemetery beside first wife Suzette. He was 67 years old. Genevieve remained a widow until her own death, at age 93, in 1955. A man of many talents and universally liked, Prior is remembered, along with his brothers-in-law, where his first wife's family farmed when Victoria was young.

LOTBINIÈRE AVENUE

Courteous and non-controversial lieut.-governor

How many times have you walked or driven past Government House and hardly noticed the narrow lane that marks its western border? A stroll along that lane is full of surprises. Close to Rockland Avenue, an iron gate and gateposts in the stone wall frame a unique view of the pretty garden on Government House's western side. Farther down, a peek over the same wall reveals buttercups, an unrestrained carpet of colour that contrasts nicely with the manicured splendour of the formal gardens. A few yards on, rocky prominences rear up beyond the wall, with part of the mansion visible on the hill behind them. Trees line the section of the lane that snakes down to Richardson Street. All is peaceful here. The scents of nature tickle your nose. Birdsong fills your ears.

The lane is named after British Columbia's seventh lieutenant-governor, Sir Henri Joly de Lotbinière. Born in France and a long-time resident of Quebec, Sir Henri was the first French-Canadian appointed to the position. He was also the first to occupy the newly refurbished Government House on Rockland Avenue.

The original dwelling on that site had been erected some 40 years earlier by George Hunter Cary, attorney-general for British Columbia and Vancouver Island. Shortly after his arrival in 1859, Cary bought land from James Douglas and Joseph D. Pemberton and proceeded to build himself a small castle. Then his fortunes changed. Poor investments fostered financial ruin, and in 1865 he returned to England. His behaviour here had sometimes been irrational—he once startled onlookers by galloping across the James Bay Bridge at breakneck speed and was involved in several fights with political opponents—so Victorians were not surprised to learn that he had been stricken with insanity and died, in 1866, of "softening of the brain."

Sir Henri Joly de Lotbinière

"Cary Castle" became Government House in 1864, when Governor Arthur Edward Kennedy moved in. Several occupants and two fires later, little was left of the castle that Cary had built. Resident at the time of the second and most devastating fire was Lieutenant-Governor

Viewed from the northwest entrance gate in the 1860s, old Government House (or Cary Castle, as it was called) stood in near solitary splendour on its Rockland perch. Today, Lotbiniere Avenue runs off beyond the smaller gate at the right of this picture.

Dr. Thomas McInnes. He and his family lost personal effects, pets, and their home in the early morning of May 18, 1899. Only the ballroom and the conservatory were spared by the blaze, which was blamed on a defective flue.

McInnes and his family moved into the Green residence on Moss Street (now home to the Art Gallery of Greater Victoria) until the damage was repaired. But long before the new Government House arose, like a phoenix, from the ashes of the old, McInnes was gone, dismissed from office by Prime Minister Sir Wilfrid Laurier in June 1900 after one political skirmish too many.

When Sir Henri stepped off the *Islander* on June 29, 1900, his official residence was still in ruins, and the McInnes family was still living in the big house on Moss Street. A huge welcoming procession headed by Premier James Dunsmuir escorted the new lieutenant-governor into town. Sir Henri and his family stayed at the Driard Hotel for a while, then moved to Moss Street after the McInneses left.

Rebuilding their new home, designed and constructed under the watchful eye of noted local architects Samuel Maclure and Francis Rattenbury, took longer than anyone anticipated. Finally, in August 1903, the lieutenant-governor was able to move in. One month later, he hosted delegates to the Chamber of Commerce of the British Empire, who, according to the *Colonist*, enjoyed breakfast at the Driard Hotel, a carriage ride through town, and champagne at the Hon. Col. E.G. Prior's Pemberton Road home before visiting the lieutenant-governor's palatial new residence.

Lady Joly was in her element, able at last to entertain on a grand scale and to host the ladies' gatherings of which she was so fond. Sadly, she did not live long to enjoy this new and most thrilling time of her life. She became progressively unwell, and in August 1904 she died at the age of 67.

It was a terrible shock for Sir Henri. They had been married for 48 years. Lady Joly had borne him eleven children, six of whom, all now grown, survived to mourn her. Sir Henri took her body back to Quebec, where she was buried. He came back to Victoria, but found himself unable to reconcile his great loss. He resigned his position the following year, returned to Quebec, and died there a few years later.

He was sorely missed in Victoria. Warned by Sir Wilfrid Laurier not to follow his predecessor's footsteps, Sir Henri had been courteous, non-controversial, and a gentleman to the core. Interested in conservation and forestry, he planted several specimen trees in the Government House grounds, not far from the meandering roadway between Rockland and Richardson that now bears his name.

The Driard Hotel, on the site of today's Eaton Centre, served as a temporary home for Sir Henri and his family when they arrived in Victoria in 1900 to find Government House in ruins after a fire. They lived at the Green residence on Moss Street (now the Art Gallery of Greater Victoria) before moving into their newly built official residence in 1903.

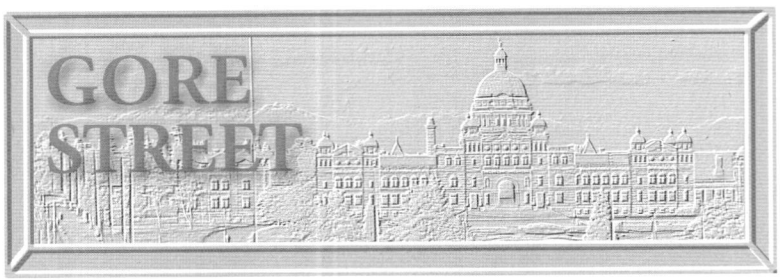

Brothers surveyed all before them

Gore Street in Esquimalt makes a fine shortcut between Lyall and Head streets near West Bay Marina. Short it certainly is—unlike the long and interesting career of the man for whom it was named in 1890. But our story starts some 50 years earlier, in 1840, when civil engineer William Sinclair Gore left Co. Antrim, Ireland, and settled with his new bride in western Ontario. He practised for a while before buying land at Rice Lake, north of Cobourg, and turning to farming. There, at what became known as Gore's Landing, near Peterborough, his two sons first saw the light of day.

The oldest, also named William Sinclair Gore, was born in 1842. He was sent to school in Ireland for several years, then attended grammar school at Barrie. Following in his father's footsteps, W.S. took a civil engineering course at the University of Toronto and served articles at Bowmanville.

By 1864 he had obtained his commission as a land surveyor and moved south of the border to work on railway surveys and construction. While in Iowa in 1868, he met and married the love of his life, Jennie Blodgett of Boston. In 1869–70, the dominion government took over control of the North West Territory from the Hudson's Bay Company, and W.S. was hired to survey all the land reserves surrounding HBC posts west of Fort Garry (now Winnipeg). Thus began his journey toward the island he would eventually call home.

After surveying land around 22 posts across the country, W.S., his wife, and their young son finally arrived in Victoria in 1875. Thirteen years after its incorporation as a city, Victoria was finally about to receive piped water from Elk Lake.

The Gores lived on the northeast corner of Burdett and Quadra. In those days the area was called Victoria Crescent, and the old Christ Church Cathedral stood where the Law Courts stand today. Their two sons, Thomas and Arthur, attended the Collegiate School, just down the hill past the cathedral, with the sons of prominent families with names like Tolmie, Barnard, and Pemberton.

Thomas Sinclair Gore

Gore Street

W.S. Gore's sons, Thomas and Arthur, attended the Collegiate School with the children of Francis Jones Barnard, whose Barnard's Express Co. was the first stage line to carry mail to the Cariboo.

W.S. was hired by the B.C. government to survey different parts of the province, and on completion of these projects he was appointed chief draughtsman in the Department of Lands and Works. By 1878 he was surveyor-general of B.C., and twelve years later was promoted to deputy commissioner of Lands and Works. He retired in 1905.

Meanwhile, W.S.'s brother T.S. (for Thomas Sinclair) had followed a similar but slightly different route to the coast. Younger than his brother by nine years, T.S. had his first experience of surveying in Iowa and Nebraska and then, like his brother, attended school in Toronto. In 1876, while W.S. was working in B.C., T.S. was articling at Lake of the Woods, making preliminary surveys for the future location of a transcontinental railroad.

Five years later and now fully qualified, he was hired by the dominion government to survey along the international boundary in the Souris River country. In 1882 he moved west and selected land for a farm near where he figured the Canadian Pacific Railway would pass. The next year he was involved with government work once more, and in 1885 served with the surveyors' intelligence corps in the Riel Rebellion. In 1887 he moved farther west, crossing the Rockies to do surveying work for the B.C. government. Central Canada would not be the same without him. The Saskatchewan Legislative Buildings stand on the site of his once-isolated prairie farm.

By 1890, when his older brother was receiving his latest promotion, T.S. was in Victoria, setting up a business in partnership

William Sinclair Gore (inset) was commodore of the Royal Victoria Yacht Club at Cadboro Bay, pictured here in 1911.

with Captain J. Herrick McGregor. Using the Gore & McGregor office as his headquarters, T.S. acted as land commissioner for the E&N Railway, then worked for both provincial and dominion governments until his retirement in 1910. Not content to rest on his laurels, he became secretary and eventually president of the Corporation of Land Surveyors of B.C. and was president of the Arts and Crafts Society for many years.

T.S., his wife Lulie, and his stepdaughter lived in a beautiful home that stands to this day, high on a rock along York Place in Oak Bay. Later they moved a couple of blocks east to a waterfront property on Beach Drive. It was here that Thomas died, aged 85, in 1937. He had outlived his brother by almost two decades.

After his 1905 retirement, W.S. also remained active. A keen sailor, canoeist, bicyclist, and golfer, he was commodore of the Victoria (later Royal Victoria) Yacht Club and designed and built two yachts that were winners in their class. He died at his Burdett Avenue home in 1919 at the age of 77. Jennie lived until 1925.

The Gore brothers worked their way across this country to make their mark. And in Esquimalt, a street near Work Point Barracks bears short testament to their long and illustrious careers.

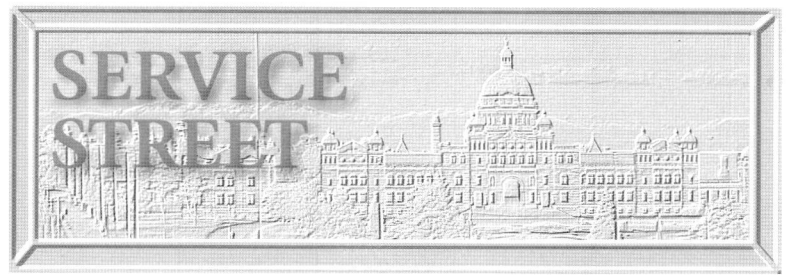

The face at the window

For the spirit-lovers amongst us, there's a street in Saanich that bears an interesting relationship to the building on the southwest corner of Government and Fort. Today that building houses a Christmas store. Yesterday, it was the home of a bank clerk who became a famous bard … and whose spirit may linger there to this day.

If he's still around, Robert William Service is a long way from his beginnings in northwestern England. He was born in Preston, Lancashire, in 1874, the first son of Robert and Emily. Four years after Robert Jr. was born, the Services moved to Scotland, the country of his father's birth. As the family grew, young Robert was sent to live with maiden aunts in Ayrshire. Here he was fussed over, indulged, and visited by his mother as often as she was able.

On one occasion when the tartan-clad youngster clambered onto her knee for a cuddle, his genteel English mother was able to confirm what she'd suspected all along—that underneath his kilt her son was as naked as the day he was born. Without further ado she removed him from his aunts' home and took him back to the bosom of his family. It was a rude awakening for Robert. One minute he was an only child; the next, he was surrounded by siblings.

Robert didn't do well in school. He enjoyed English literature—especially when it told stories of adventure—but he railed against the confines of the classroom and answered discipline with defiance. Eventually, much to his relief, he was expelled. After a few months in a shipping office, he followed his father into the banking business. Not that the work appealed to him, but it was a way to earn money for the journeys he hoped to make, and all those Bank Holidays wouldn't come amiss. Indeed, it's fortunate for us that he did become a bank clerk. If he hadn't, Victoria might never have had the pleasure of his presence.

The work was easy and the pay regular. Service recalls in his autobiography that he dallied through his day, starting late, finishing early, and making the most of every opportunity. Lunch was a leisurely half-hour break, and a trip to the bank's main branch was a chance to walk the entire distance and pocket the pennies he'd been given for the ride.

Eventually he had enough saved to board a tramp steamer and arrived in Canada with just a few dollars in his pocket. From Quebec, he took the train to the West Coast. He first set foot on Vancouver Island in 1896. In his pocket was an introduction to a fellow in Someros who was the cousin of a Glasgow friend.

Before moving to Victoria to resume his banking career, Robert Service served as a post office clerk in this Cowichan Valley store, pictured in the 1930s. In his spare time, Service penned the first of the poems that eventually brought him fame.

Service had his sights set on being a cowboy, but ended up on a farm and quickly learned that life as a lowly farmhand was a far cry from his boyhood as a banker's son. It was a hard life for a soft city-dweller, but he had something here that he prized above all else—his freedom. He persevered ... until the prospect of another West Coast winter sent him scurrying south. Later, in his autobiography *Ploughman of the Moon*, Service admitted that although each passing season held its own charm, "I could never reconcile myself to working in the rain."

He wandered around California and Mexico, but eventually made his way back up the coast. By the fall of 1898 he was in Duncan, first as a farmhand, then as a clerk in a Cowichan post office and store. He threw himself into the social scene, learning how to strum a banjo, taking part in amateur theatricals, and delighting in reciting his never-ending rhymes.

This was a turning point, for in his spare time he penned the first of several poems. The characters he had rubbed shoulders with over the years formed the bones of the verses he wrote, and he covered them with the flesh of his words. His poems were published in the *Colonist* and the *Cowichan Leader*. It was a small but significant beginning.

Service Street

In the early 1900s, the Bank of Commerce, where Robert Service worked, was one of eight financial establishments along Government Street. A look up either side of this imposing 1885 "concrete" structure shows that it is, in fact, a brick building. It was faced with cast iron and treated to look like concrete, presumably to imply permanence and inspire trust. Converted to a Christmas shop, it stands on the southwest corner of Government and Fort streets to this day.

Inside the impressive corner entrance, the bank's lofty ceilings were designed to inspire awe and—hopefully—a predisposition toward large deposits into its vaults. A room on the bank's upper floor served as Robert Service's home until 1903, when he moved to B.C.'s Interior.

Bank of Commerce staff in Dawson, Yukon, 1905. Robert Service is standing in the middle of the group in front of the window.

By the time he was 29, Service was tired of being a drifter and yearned for a more secure existence. He fancied himself a scholar, but university was not for him—he failed the entrance exams—and he decided against a college career. There was nothing for it but to go back to banking. Rusty but ready to re-learn, he applied to the Canadian Bank of Commerce and was sent to its city branch, a building on Government Street that had opened for business twenty years earlier on the site of the first Legislative Assembly at Fort Victoria. One of the perks of the $50-a-month post was free accommodation on the bank's upper floor.

He was transferred to Kamloops, then to Whitehorse, and, four years later, to Dawson City. Victoria's loss was the Yukon's gain. Service thrived in the wild winter darkness, taking up his pen once more. Of all the rhymes he wrote, two tipped the balance. The first was "The Shooting of Dan McGrew." Reading over what he'd written, he decided he didn't like it and tucked it into a desk drawer. Then one night he was inspired again. Borrowing a name from a bank ledger, he created "The Cremation of Sam McGee."

It was his Dawson writing success that

brought the financial freedom he longed for, and in 1909 he resigned from the bank to concentrate on his writing. In all, Service produced 28 books—novels, poems, and autobiographies—including *Songs of a Sourdough* (later known as *Spell of the Yukon*), *The Trail of Ninety-eight*, and *Rhymes of a Rolling Stone*.

Service was working as a newspaper correspondent in France in 1913 when he met Germaine Bourgoin. They settled in Brittany and had a daughter, Iris. Moving several times, they eventually settled in Monte Carlo and it was here, in 1958, that Service died.

And what of the ghost on Government Street? The Old Cemeteries Society's book *Favourite Ghost Stories* tells the tale of Lily, who lived and worked as a weaver on the second floor of what used to be the Albion Hotel, opposite the old Bank of Commerce, long after Service's time. Lily reckoned she was being watched by a man standing in a window across the street. Her students saw him too. But when police investigated, they found that the staircase to the bank's third floor was thick with dust. So were the rooms where bank employees had once resided. There was not a footprint in sight. It was clear that no living soul had climbed that staircase in years. Lily, they decided, was losing it. Imagining things. Seeing a man who wasn't there.

As far as we know, Robert Service spent the best part of a decade on Vancouver Island, then moved to the Yukon and never returned to B.C.

Or did he?

Nobody seems to have noticed his presence around Cowichan Bay or along the Saanich street that bears his name. But they do say he haunts the cabin where he lived in Dawson. And Lily swore that she saw a man in his apartment above the bank on Government Street

If you're ever downtown of an evening, take a look at the upper floor windows of the old bank building at Government and Fort. Maybe, like Lily, you too will see … the man who isn't there.

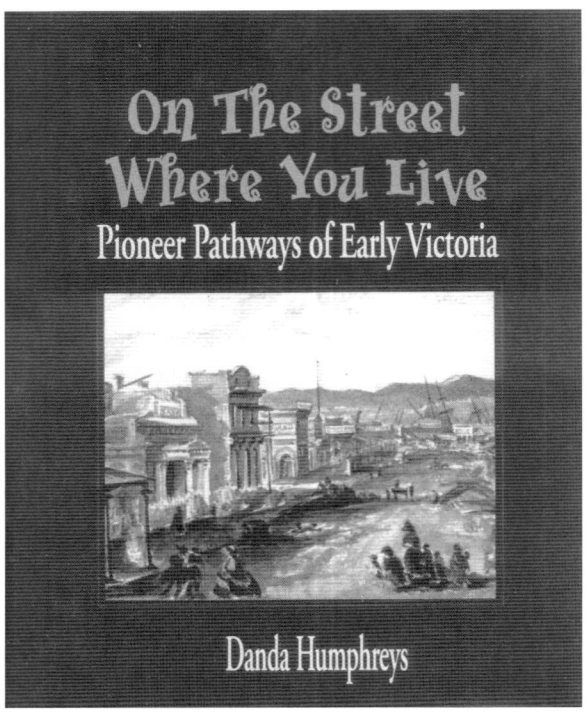

Location of Streets Included in Volume I

On The Street Where You Live: Pioneer pathways of early Victoria (Volume I in the trilogy) describes the earliest history of the city through the people its streets are named after—Hudson's Bay Company traders, farmers, politicians, lawmen, and merchants who arrived on these shores between the 1840s and 1860s. It tells of life at a frontier fort, describes the gold rush-related population boom that ensured Victoria's survival, and includes the social and political shenanigans that turned the remote colonial settlement into a vital, growing centre. The streets included in Volume I are listed at right, and their locations are indicated on the following maps.

Maps are provided for information only. They are not to scale and do not include all the streets.

Code for Maps Volume I

1	Quadra Street	page 15
2	Douglas Street	page 18
3	Fort Street	page 22
4	Blanshard Street	page 28
5	Grant Road	page 33
6	Tod Road	page 37
7	Helmcken Road	page 40
8	Pemberton Road	page 44
9	Wark Street	page 47
10	Finlayson Street	page 52
11	Macaulay Street	page 56
12	Langford Street	page 59
13	Skinner Street	page 63
14	Craigflower Road	page 67
15	Admirals Road	page 73
16	Bilston Place	page 76
17	Sooke Road	page 80
18	William Head Road	page 84
19	Cheeseman Road	page 89
20	Mount Newton Cross Road	page 93
21	Thomson Road	page 96
22	Lidgate Court	page 99
23	Dean Avenue	page 102
24	Marifield Avenue	page 105
25	Cedar Hill Road	page 110
26	Tolmie Avenue	page 118
27	Yates Street	page 121
28	Burdett Avenue	page 124
29	Beacon Street	page 128
30	Ross Street	page 132
31	Academy Close	page 137
32	McNeill Avenue	page 142
33	Fernwood Road	page 145
34	Begbie Street	page 149
35	Trutch Street	page 154
36	Pleasant Street	page 159
37	Pentrelew Place	page 165
38	Regents Place	page 170
39	Maynard Street	page 174
40	Carr Street	page 178

Location of Streets in Volume I

Victoria and Outlying Areas

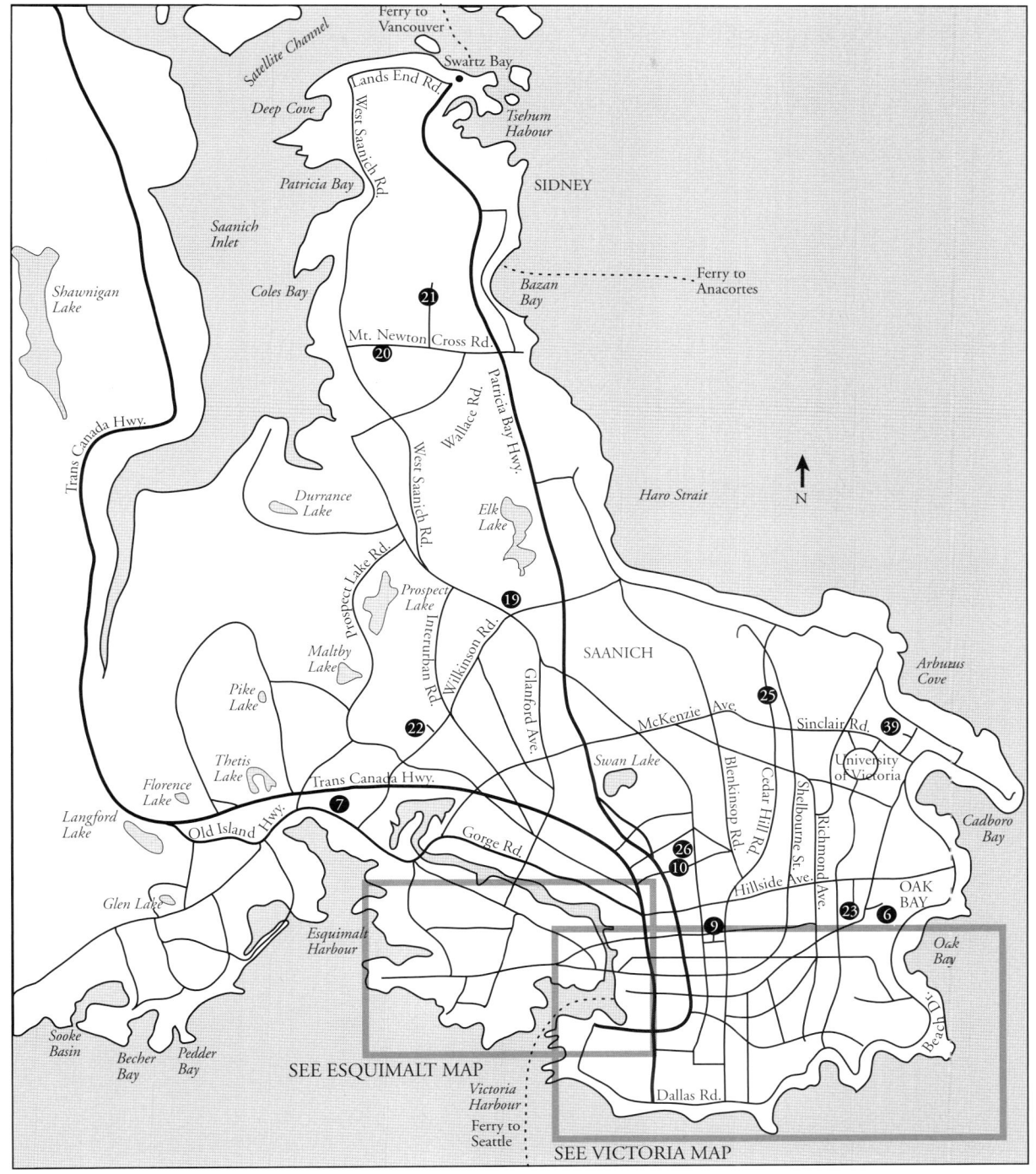

On the Street Where You Live

Victoria and Oak Bay

Esquimalt

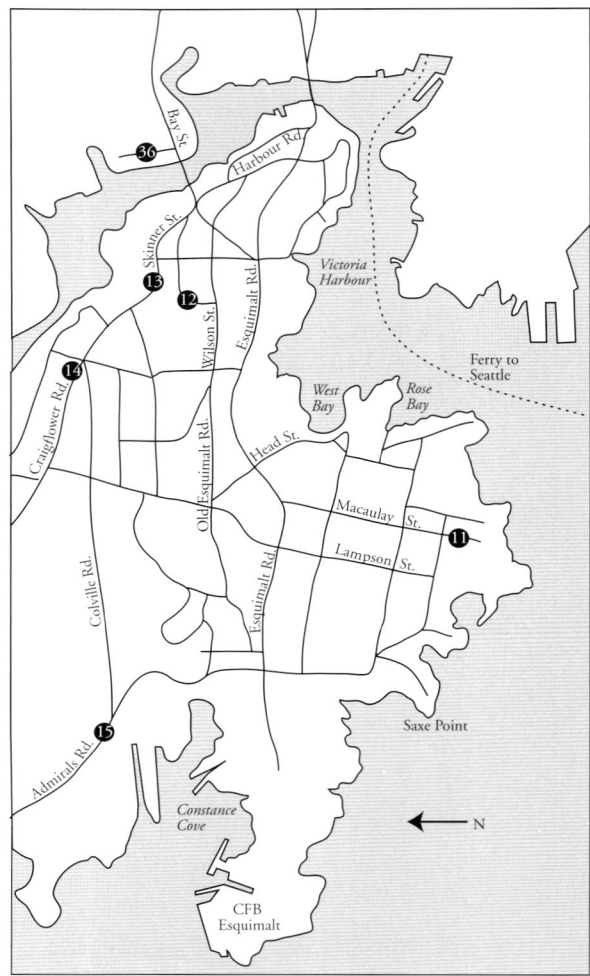

Sooke and Metchosin

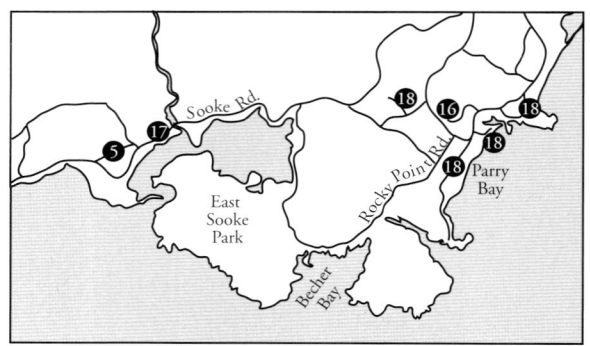

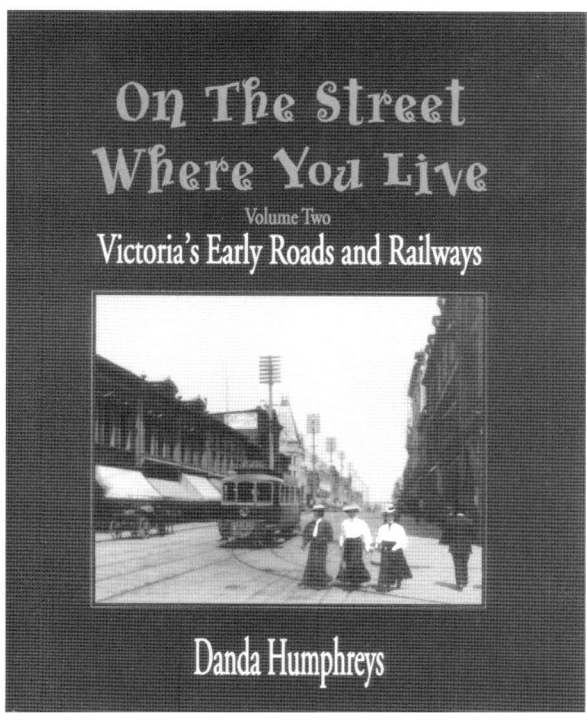

Location of Streets Included in Volume II

On The Street Where You Live: Victoria's early roads and railways (Volume II in the trilogy) tells how the city grew, in the mid-1860s, from a fur trading post into a provincial capital—the jewel in British Columbia's golden crown. Danda introduces us to some of the men and women who were drawn to the growing city from the 1860s on. She takes us on another step back in time, along the roads and railways that connected the original city core to today's suburbs, forging a vital link between the downtown area and distant communities. The streets included in Volume II are listed at right, and their locations are indicated on the following maps.

Maps are provided for information only. They are not to scale and do not include all the streets.

Code for Maps Volume II

1	Bastion Square	page 12
2	Rowland Avenue	page 16
3	Harris Green	page 19
4	Waddington Alley	page 23
5	Carberry Gardens	page 27
6	Hayward Heights	page 30
7	Fell Street	page 35
8	Shotbolt Road	page 38
9	Dingley Dell	page 41
10	Davie Street	page 47
11	Langley Street	page 52
12	Joan Crescent	page 55
13	Burleith Crescent	page 60
14	Weiler Avenue	page 66
15	Wilspencer Place	page 70
16	Richardson	page 76
17	Munro Street	page 80
18	Rithet Street	page 84
19	Irving Road	page 88
20	Government Street	page 91
21	Campbell's Corner	page 96
22	Veyaness Road	page 100
23	Christmas Avenue	page 107
24	Royal Oak Drive	page 110
25	East Saanich Road	page 114
26	Sidney Avenue	page 118
27	Iroquois Way	page 123
28	Interurban Road	page 127
29	Marigold Road	page 131
30	Wilkinson Road	page 135
31	Eberts Street and Goward Road	page 139
32	Stevens Road	page 143
33	Prospect Lake Road	page 147
34	Sluggett Avenue	page 150
35	Stelly's Cross Road	page 154
36	Tatlow Road	page 157
37	Canora Road	page 161
38	Lochside Drive	page 164
39	Alpha Street	page 168
40	Edward Milne Road	page 173

On the Street Where You Live

Victoria and outlying areas

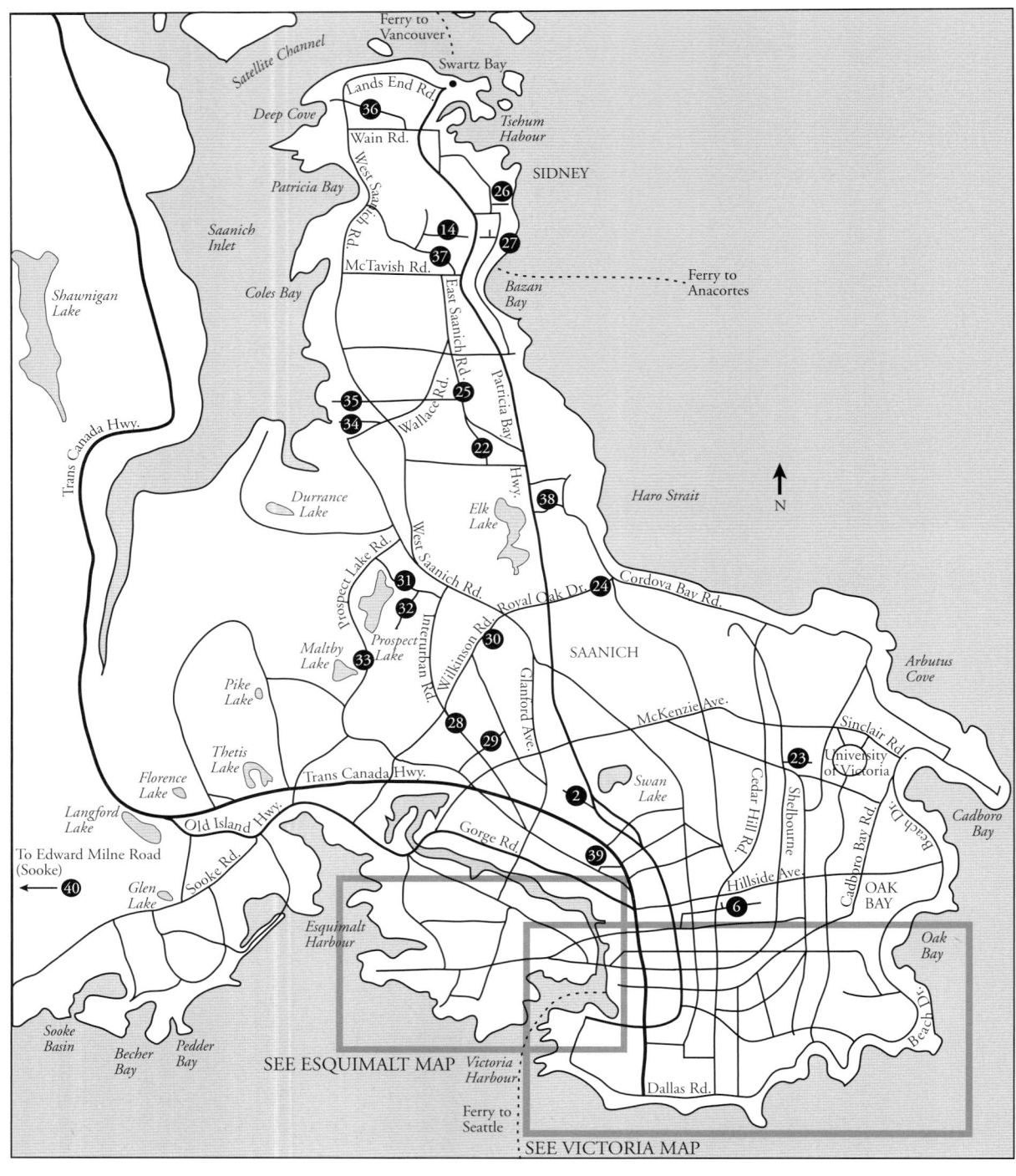

Location of Streets in Volume II

Victoria and Oak Bay

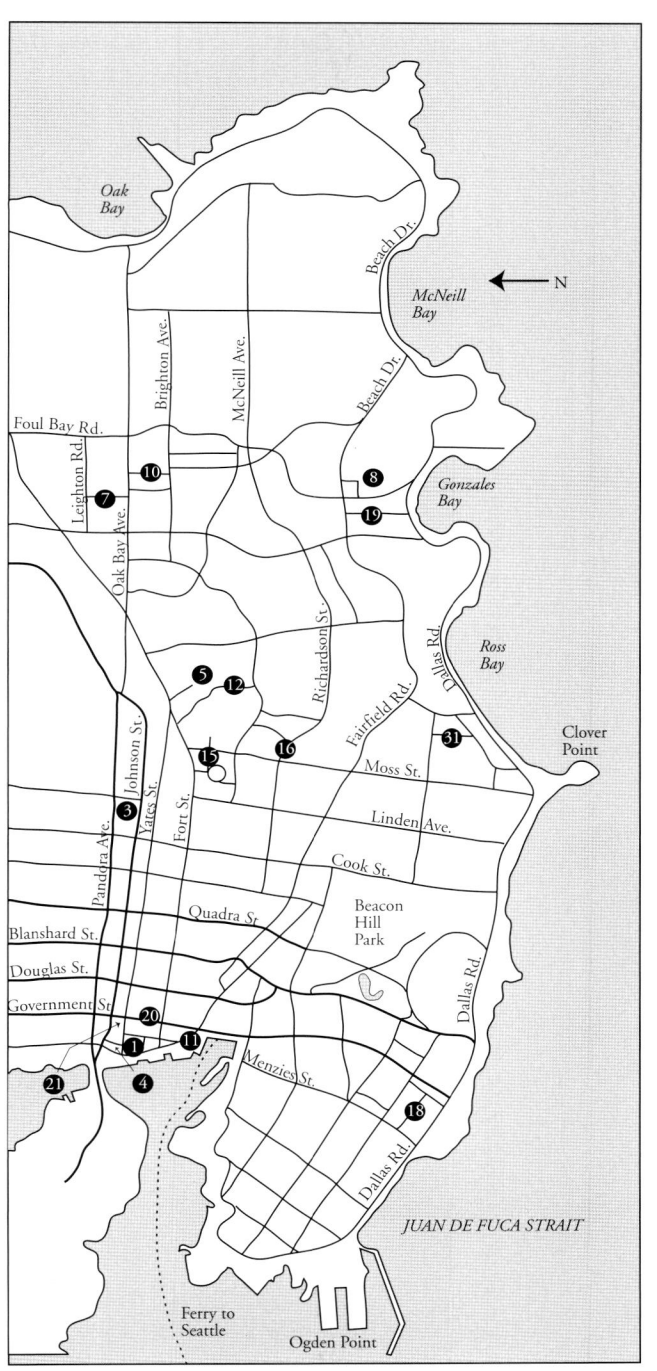

Esquimalt

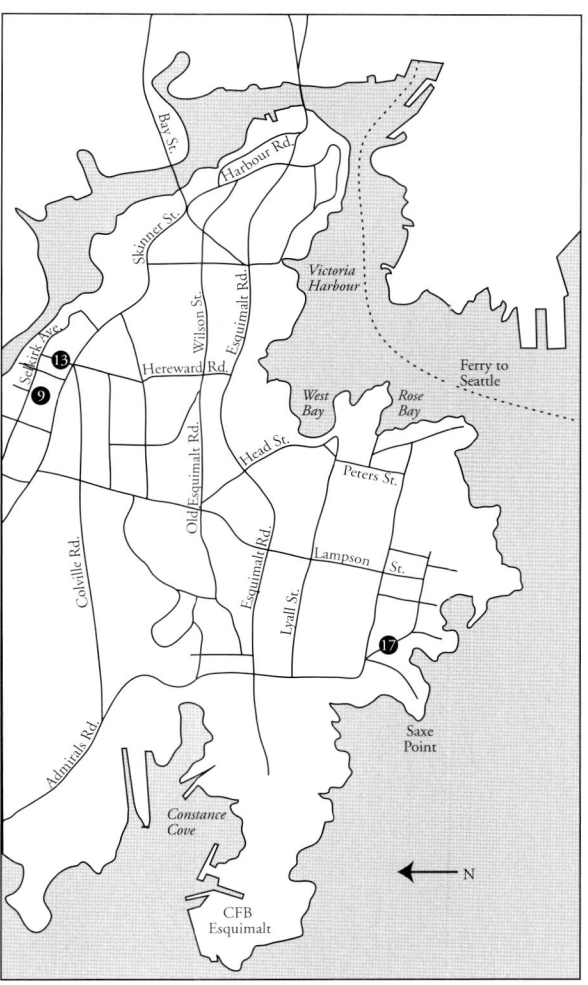

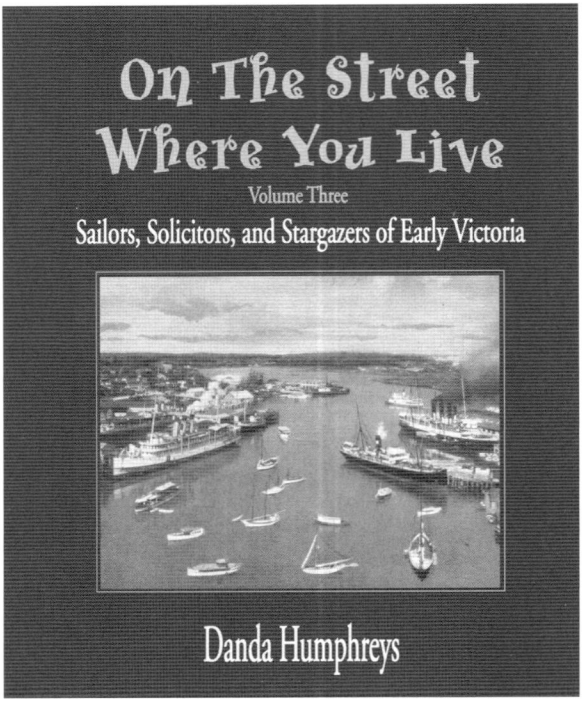

Location of Streets Included in Volume III

On The Street Where You Live: Sailors, solicitors and stargazers of early Victoria (Volume III in the trilogy) introduces us to more of the colourful characters who were drawn to the city during the second half of the nineteenth century. The bare bones of our city's beginnings, muscled by farmers and men of fortune, are fleshed out by an interesting cast of characters including sailors and saloon-keepers, lawyers, bankers and businessmen, architects and astronomers, doctors, politicians, postmasters, even a poet or two. The streets included in Volume III are listed at right, and their locations are indicated on the following maps.

Maps are provided for information only. They are not to scale and do not include all the streets.

Code for Maps Volume III

1	Cadboro Bay Road	page 11
2	Old Esquimalt Road	page 16
3	Esquimalt Road	page 19
4	Thetis Lane	page 2
5	Race Passage Close	page 25
6	Walbran Park	page 28
7	Rudlin Street	page 31
8	Sayward Street	page 35
9	Fan Tan Alley	page 38
10	Powell Street	page 42
11	Tiedemann Place	page 46
12	Trounce Alley	page 49
13	Wilson Street	page 54
14	Hibbens Close	page 57
15	Redfern Street	page 60
16	Goodacre Lake	page 64
17	Carroll Street	page 69
18	Dallas Road	page 73
19	Bushby Street	page 77
20	Franklin Terrace	page 80
21	Belmont Road	page 83
22	Young Street	page 86
23	Elliott Street	page 89
24	Pooley Street	page 92
25	Mystic Lane	page 95
26	Shakespeare Street	page 98
27	Pendray Street	page 102
28	Rattenbury Place	page 106
29	Maclure Road	page 111
30	Courtney Street	page 116
31	Paul Kane Place	page 120
32	Sangster Lane	page 124
33	Denison Road	page 127
34	Hastings Street	page 131
35	Harrison Street	page 134
36	Point Street	page 137
37	Medana Street	page 143
38	Earle Street	page 147
39	Prior Street	page 151
40	Lotbiniere Avenue	page 155
41	Gore Street	page 158
42	Service Street	page 161

Location of Streets in Volume III

Victoria and outlying areas

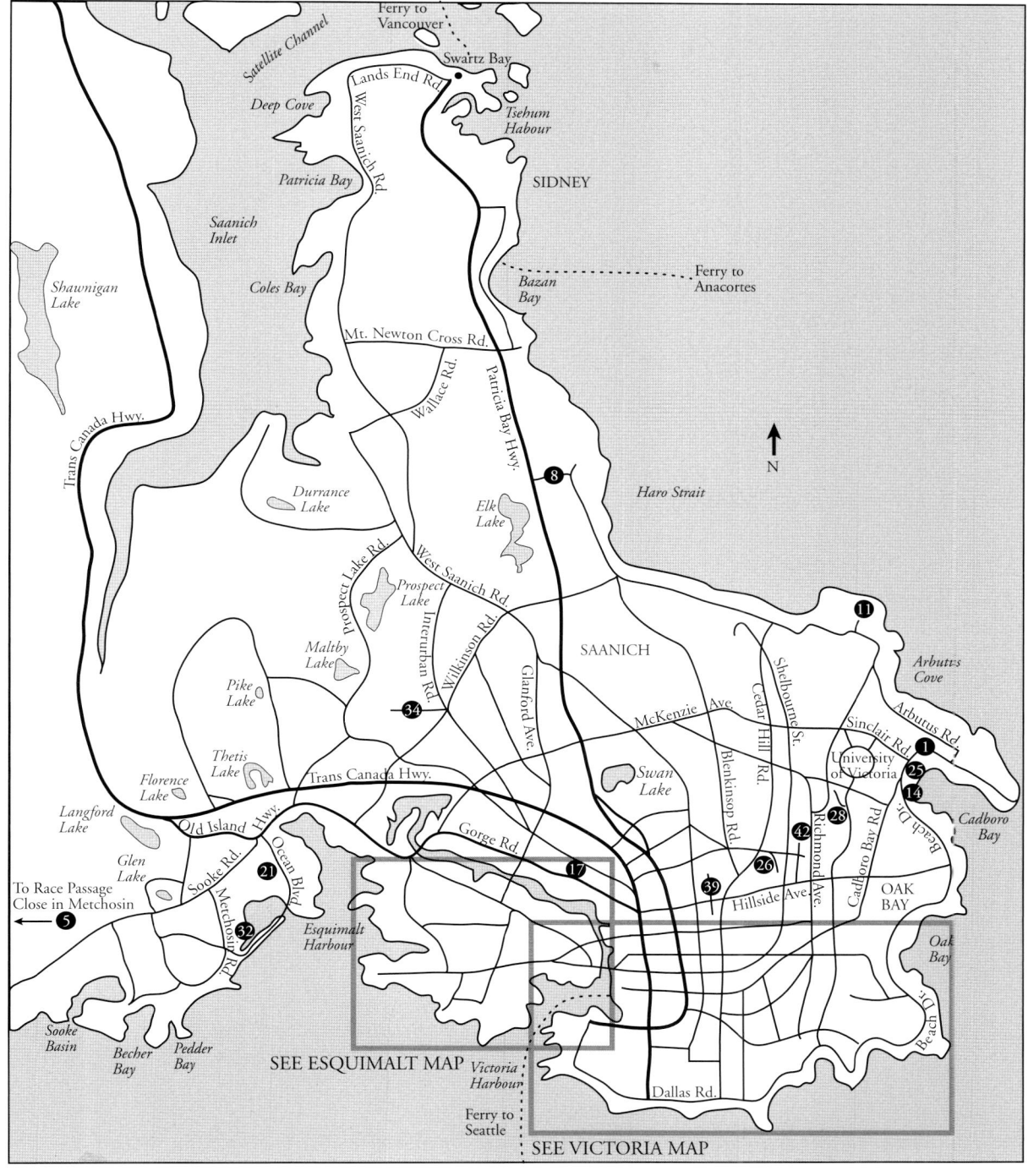

On the Street Where You Live

Victoria and Oak Bay

Esquimalt

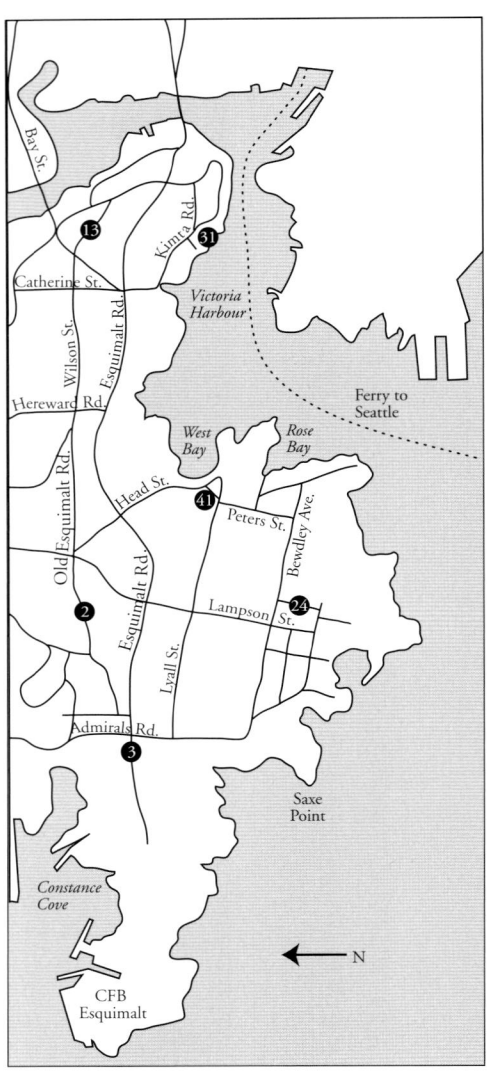

Bibliography

Source material at the British Columbia Archives and Records Service, City of Victoria Archives, Saanich Municipal Archives, Esquimalt Municipal Archives, Saanich Pioneer Society, Sooke Region Museum, and the Greater Victoria Public Library was supplemented with information from the following books, as well as from the *Victoria Times Colonist*, newspapers of the News Group, and the July/August 1981 edition of The *Northwestern Review* (Seattle, WA), with its page 22 article on the Saywards.

Akrigg, G.P.V. and Helen B. Akrigg. *British Columbia Chronicle 1847-1871: Gold & colonists*. Vancouver, BC: Discovery Press, 1977.

Barnes, Fred C. (ed.). *Only In Oak Bay: Oak Bay Municipality 1906-1981*. Victoria, BC: The Corporation of the District of Oak Bay, 1981.

Barr, Jennifer Nell. *Saanich Heritage Structures: An inventory*. Victoria, BC: Corporation of the District of Saanich, 1991.

Baskerville, Peter A. *Beyond the Island: An illustrated history of Victoria*. Burlington, ON: Windsor Publications Ltd., 1986.

Bingham, Janet. *Samuel Maclure, Architect*. Ganges, BC: Horsdal and Schubart, 1985.

British Columbia From The Earliest Times To The Present, Biographical Vol. IV. Vancouver, BC: The S.J. Clarke Publishing Company, 1914.

Castle, Geoffrey (ed.). *Saanich: An illustrated history*. Sidney, BC: Manning Press, 1989.

Cotton, Peter. *Vice Regal Mansions of British Columbia*. Vancouver, BC: Elgin Publications Ltd., 1981.

Downs, Art (ed.). *Pioneer Days in British Columbia*, Vol. 2. Surrey, BC: Heritage House, 1975.

Duffus, Maureen (ed.). *Craigflower Country: A history of View Royal 1850-1950*. Victoria, BC: Desktop Publishing Ltd., 1993.

Eaton, Diane and Sheila Urbanek. *Paul Kane's Great Nor-West*. Vancouver, BC: UBC Press, 1995.

Fawcett, Edgar. *Some Reminiscences of Old Victoria*. Toronto, ON: William Briggs, 1912.

Grant, Peter. *Victoria: A history in photographs*. Canmore, AB: Altitude Publishing Canada Ltd., 1995.

Green, Valerie. *No Ordinary People*. Victoria, BC: Beach Holme Publishers, 1992.

Higgins, David Williams. *Tales of a Pioneer Journalist: From gold rush to Government*

Street in 19th century Victoria. Downs, Art (ed.). Surrey, BC: Heritage House, 1996.

———. *The Passing of a Race*. Toronto: Wm. Briggs, 1904.

Humphreys, Danda. *Favourite Ghost Stories from the tours of The Old Cemeteries Society*. Victoria, BC: The Old Cemeteries Society, 1997.

———. *Favourite Stories from Lantern Tours in the Old Burying Ground*. Victoria, BC: The Old Cemeteries Society, 1998.

———. *On The Street Where You Live, Volume I: Pioneer Pathways of Early Victoria*. Surrey, BC: Heritage House, 1999.

———. *On The Street Where You Live, Volume II: Victoria's Early Roads and Railways*. Surrey, BC: Heritage House, 2000.

Isenor, D.E., W.N. McInnis, E.G. Stephens, and D.E. Watson. *The Land of Plenty*. Campbell River, BC: Ptarmigan Press, 1987.

Jupp, Ursula. *Cadboro: A ship, a bay, a sea-monster*. Victoria, BC: Ursula Jupp Estate, 1988.

Kane, Paul. *Wanderings of an Artist Among the Indians of North America*. Mineola, NY: Dover Publications Inc., 1996.

Kluckner, Michael. *Victoria: The Way It Was*. North Vancouver, BC: Whitecap Books, 1986.

Lai, David Chuenyan. *The Forbidden City Within Victoria*. Victoria, BC: Orca Books, 1991.

Minaker, Dennis. *The Gorge Of Summers Gone*. Victoria, BC: Desktop Publishing Limited, 1998.

Nicholson, George. *Vancouver Island's West Coast, 1762-1962*. Victoria, BC: Morriss Printing Company Limited, 1962.

Ormsby, Margaret A. *British Columbia: A history*. Toronto, ON: Macmillan, 1958.

Page, Bess. *Metchosin Names: A history of the place names in Metchosin*. Victoria, BC: Bess Page, 2000.

Pearson, Anne. *Sea–Lake: Recollections and History of Cordova Bay and Elk Lake*. Victoria, BC: Sea–Lake Editions, 1981.

Peers, Elida. *The Sooke Story: The history and the heartbeat*. Sooke, BC: Sooke Region Museum, 1999.

Rayner, William. *British Columbia's Premiers in Profile*. Surrey, BC: Heritage House, 2000.

Reksten, Terry. *Rattenbury*. Victoria, BC: Sono Nis Press, 1978.

Robinson, Leigh Burpee. *Esquimalt: "Place of Shoaling Waters."* Victoria, BC: Quality Press, 1947.

Robinson, Sherri K. *Esquimalt Streets and Roads: A history*. Victoria, BC: Sherri K. Robinson, 1995.

Segger, Martin and Douglas Franklin. *Exploring Victoria's Architecture*. Victoria, BC: Sono Nis Press, 1996.

Smith, Dorothy Blakey (ed.). *The Reminiscences of Doctor John Sebastian Helmcken*. Vancouver, BC: UBC Press, 1975.

This Old House: An Inventory of Residential Heritage. Victoria, BC: City of Victoria, 1979.

Walbran, John T. *British Columbia Coast Names 1592-1906: Their origin and history*. North Vancouver, BC: J.J. Douglas Ltd., 1971.

Ward, Robin. *Echoes of Empire: Victoria and its remarkable buildings*. Madeira Park, BC: Harbour Publishing, 1996.

INDEX

Admirals Road 17
Adriatic 151
Akrigg, G.P.V. 29
Albert Head 139
Amateur Dramatic Association 81
Anglo-American Hotel 42
Argyle Avenue 27
Argyle Place 27
Argyle, Albert 27
Argyle, Anne 26
Argyle, Ellen 26
Argyle, Frederick 26
Argyle, Grace 26
Argyle, Helen 27
Argyle, Jenny 26
Argyle, Louisa 26
Argyle, Mary Ellen 26-27
Argyle, Maude 26
Argyle, Thomas 26-27
Argyle, Thomas Jr. 27
"Armadale" 52
Art Gallery of Greater Victoria 156, 157
B.C. Medical Council 44
Bank of British Columbia 163
Bank of Montreal 100
Barkerville 54, 111
Barkley Sound 29
Barkley, Charles William 29
Barkley, Frances 29
Barnard, Francis Jones 159
Bastion Street 48, 51, 59
Beacon Hill 11, 24, 75, 124
Beacon Hill Park 49, 50, 67, 68, 75-76, 137, 153
Beaver 24, 32, 75, 124, 125
Beckley Farm 144
Bedford Regency Hotel 59
Begbie, Matthew Baillie 77-78, 79, 92
Belcher Street 132
"Belmont" 83, 84, 85, 87
Belmont Building 129, 130

Belmont Point 85
Belmont Street 85
Beresford, Charles 19
Bexley Farm 144
Billings Point 137
Billings, William Thomas 137
Birdcage Walk 67, 90
Birdcages 9, 46-47, 107, 143
Bissett, James 47
Black Diamond 31
Bland, Elizabeth 20
Bland, James 20
Blanshard, Richard 131
Bolduc, J. 95
Bone, W.H. 59
Book of Small 58
Booth, Julia 96-97
Boyd Street 146
British America Paint Company 104-105
British Astronomical Association 132
British Columbia: colony of 26, 74, 77, 87, 90, 111; merged with Vancouver Island 64, 82, 85, 88, 90, 111; Confederation 28, 43-44, 112
British Columbia Coast Names 29-30, 31, 116
British Columbia Soap Works 103
Britten, R.F. 17
Brotchie Ledge 112
Brotchie, William 12, 13
Brother Jonathan 135
Brown Jug Saloon 55, 69-71
Brown, Peter 24
Bucket of Blood. *See* Esquimalt Hotel.
Bulwer-Lytton, Edward 89
Burpee, Lawrence 120
Bushby Street 77, 79
Bushby, Agnes 79
Bushby, Agnes Douglas 77, 78-79
Bushby, Annie 79
Bushby, Arthur 79
Bushby, Arthur Thomas 77-79, 81, 85

Bushby, Ella 79
Bushby, George 79
Cadboro 11-15, 124
Cadboro Bay 11-13, 15, 95-97, 131, 160
Cadboro Bay Beach Hotel 96
Cadboro Bay Road 7, 14, 15, 95, 132, 148
Calder, Alexander 118
Cameron Lake 85
Cameron, Cecilia Douglas Cowan 83-85, 87
Cameron, David 82, 83-85
Canadian Bank of Commerce 164
Canadian Pacific 30, 34, 44, 104, 159
Canadian Pacific Navigation Company 28, 32, 34
Cape Anne 30
Carey, Joseph 118
Cariboo Fly 32
Cariboo gold rush 54, 132, 147
Cariboo Wagon Road 111, 132
Carr, Emily 32, 39, 58
Carr, Richard 47, 50
Carroll Street 72
Carroll, Adele 71
Carroll, Ellen 71
Carroll, John D. 69-72
Carswell, James 57, 58
"Cary Castle" 155-156. *See also* Government House.
Cary, George Hunter 155
Cattle Point 13, 137
Cedar Hill Cross Road 95
cemeteries 38, 82, 145-146
Centennial Square 38
Centennial United Church 101
CFB Esquimalt 19, 21
Chambers Street 32, 36
Chambers, James 36
Chambers, Walter 36
Charles E. Redfern 63
Charmer 32-33
Chew 39
Chinatown 38, 39-40
Chinese people 38-41, 100
Chinese Cemetery 41
Chinese Point. *See* Harling Point.
Christ Church Cathedral 158
Christie Point 137
Christie, John 137
Clallam people 11, 13
Cleo 19
Clover Point 128, 141

Clover Street 141
Coach and Horses 19
Coleman, Edmund T. 138
Collegiate School 158, 159
Collinson Street 115
Collinson, Richard 115
Colonist 40, 42, 44, 47, 57, 65, 72, 85, 87, 88, 91, 94, 117, 127, 146, 149, 157, 162
Colonist Printing and Publishing Co. 94
Columbia 31
Colwood 125
Commodore 74
Congregation Emanu-El 81
Constance 116, 117
Constance Cove Farm 17, 117
Cooper, James 25
Cormorant 137
Cormorant Point 137
Counting House 52
Courtenay 119
Courtenay River 119
Courtenay, George William Conway 116-117, 119, 120
Courtney Street 116, 119
Courtney, Arthur 118, 119
Courtney, Ethel 119
Courtney, Henry Classon 116, 117-119
Courtney, Knox 118, 119
Courtney, Mary Jane Calder 116, 118-119
Cowichan Leader 162
Cowichan people 24
Cowichan Valley 5, 63, 162
Cowlitz 124
Craigdarroch Castle 52
Craigflower Farm 17, 137
Crease, Sarah 39
Cridge, Edward 29, 87, 90
Customs House 99
Cutler, Lyman 75
Dakota 91
Dallas Mountain 76
Dallas Road 30, 73, 74, 76
Dallas, Alexander 78
Dallas, Alexander Grant 73-76
Dallas, James Douglas. 76
Dallas, Jane Douglas 73, 74, 76, 78
Dallas, Rupert 73
Davie, A.E.B. 94
Davie, Theodore 94, 135

Index

Davies, George 25, 47
Dawson City 164
Day, John 19
De Cosmos, Amor 47, 85, 87, 88, 99
de Lopez de Haro, Gonzalo 16
de Lotbiniere, Henri Joly 155, 156-157
de Lotbiniere, Lady Joly 157
Dean, James 11
Deluge Fire Department 44
Denison Road 127, 130
Denison, Ethel Margaret Walbran 129-130
Denison, Francis Napier 5, 127-130, 131, 133
Diocese of British Columbia 45
Discovery 31, 35
Discovery Island 31, 34
Dominion Meteorological Service 128, 130
Doughty, Edith Cameron 83, 85
Doughty, Henry 85
Douglas, Amelia 90
Douglas, James 9, 13, 16, 23-24, 28, 46, 73-74, 77-78, 79, 83-85, 86-88, 89, 90, 111, 117, 121, 124, 131, 139, 143, 155
Douglas, James William 90-91
Douglas, Mary Rachael Elliott 89, 90-91
Driard Hotel 156
Duncan 162
Dunsmuir, James 114, 135, 154, 156
Dunsmuir, Joan 135
Dunsmuir, Robert 52, 99
E&N Railway 160
E.G. Prior & Co. 153
Earle Street 150
Earle, Lizzie 147
Earle, Thomas 147-150
earthquakes 128
Eaton Centre 55, 157
Edith Point 85
Edward VII 21
Elk Lake 37, 48
Ellice Point 137
Ellice, Edward 137
Elliott Street 89, 91
Elliott, Andrew Charles 89-91, 92
Elliott, Marie 115
Elliott, Mary 89, 90-91
Emily Harris 48, 99
Emma 31
Empress Hotel 30, 68, 76, 103, 104, 108, 109, 129
Enterprise 115

"Erin Hall" 37
Esquimalt 16-21, 23, 92-94, 117, 131, 139
Esquimalt Harbour 16-17, 24, 25, 27, 47, 51, 87, 95, 116
Esquimalt Hotel 19
Esquimalt Road 16, 19-21, 93
Esquimalt Waterworks 94
Ethel Island 30
Evans, Benjamin 12
Fan Tan Alley 38, 40-41
Favourite Ghost Stories 165
Fawcett, Edgar 58, 97, 98, 101
Fawcett, Thomas 49
Fell, James 58
Fellows, Alfred 152
"Fernhill" 93
Fields, Pete 66
Finlayson Building 48
5th Regiment Garrison Artillery 152, 153
Finlayson Point 137
Finlayson, Roderick 117, 121, 137, 151
Finlayson, Sarah Work 151
Finnerty, Michael 12, 142
fire department 44, 63, 71-72
Fisgard Island 25
Fisgard Island lighthouse 27, 47
Fisher, William 92
Flathead Indians 121
Florence Island 30
Fort Langley 11
Fort Macaulay 20
Fort Rodd Hill 20, 84
Fort Street 49, 126, 132, 148
Fort Vancouver 11, 14, 28, 121, 124, 139
Fort Victoria 9, 13, 15, 28, 46, 70, 73, 86, 116-117, 121, 124, 126, 131, 137, 143, 150
Foul Bay 141
Fox, Cecil 113
Franklin & Co. 81
Franklin Terrace 82
Franklin, John 82, 115
Franklin, Lumley 80-82
Franklin, Selim 80-82, 83
Fraser Canyon 77-78, 132
The Fraser Mines Vindicated 57
Fraser River gold rush 18, 19, 31, 35, 38, 46, 69, 74, 77-78, 125
Fulford, John 25
Ganges 25

Glenlyon School 109
Gold Harbour 23
Gonzales Bay 141
Gonzales Hill 28, 128
Gonzales Weather Station 127-131
Good, Alice Douglas 78
Good, Charles 78
Goodacre Lake 67, 68
Goodacre, Lawrence 64-68
Goodacre, Maria Stafford 64-65, 67-68
Goodacre, Roy 66
Goodacre, Sam 66
Gordon, G.T. 137
Gore Street 158, 160
Gore, Arthur 158, 159
Gore, Jennie Blodgett 158, 160
Gore, Lulie 160
Gore, Thomas 158, 159
Gore, Thomas Sinclair 159-160
Gore, William Sinclair 158-160
Gore, William Sinclair Sr. 158
Government House 109, 113, 153, 154, 155-157. *See also* "Cary Castle."
Government Street 49, 55, 60, 62, 63, 67, 69-70, 82, 104, 126, 163
Government Street clock 62, 63
Granville. *See* Vancouver.
Grappler 31
Green Building 52
Halfway House 20
Harling Point 41, 137
Harling, Fred 137
Harris, Thomas 42, 58, 64, 82
Harrison Street 134, 135, 136
Harrison, Agnes 135
Harrison, Eli Jr. 134, 135-136
Harrison, Eli Sr. 134-136
Harrison, Elizabeth Warburton 134-136
Harrison, Eunice Seabrook 135-136
Harrison, George 134-135
Harrison, John 134-135
Harrison, William 134
Hastings Street 133
Hastings, Matilda Birch 132
Hastings, Oregon Columbus 131-133
Hastings, Silvestria Theodora Layzell Smith 132-133
Hatley Park 114
Haverfield, John Turnstall 117
Head Street 20

Helgesen Point 137
Hell's Gate Canyon 78
Helmcken House 91
Helmcken, Cecilia Douglas 78, 83
Helmcken, J.S. 29, 73, 78, 83, 85, 89, 91, 124, 125
Herald 25, 137
Hibben, Janet Parker Brown 58, 59
Hibben, Thomas 60
Hibben, Thomas Napier 57-59
Hibben-Bone Building 59
Hibbens Close 59
Higgins, D.W. 96
Highrock Park 25
Hill, John 151
Hillside Farm 151
Hobbs, Edwin 12
Holland Point 143
Home for Aged and Infirm Women 67
Hooper, Thomas 149
Hotel Dallas 56, 76
Hotel Willows 14
Hudson's Bay Company 11, 13-14, 16, 23-24, 25, 29, 73-75, 76, 121, 124, 126, 137, 139, 144, 158
Hudson's Bay Company Archives 125
Imperial Eagle 29
Inskip, G.H. 29
Investigator 115
Irving, John 32, 50, 51
Islander 32, 34, 156
Jacobson, Minnie 20
Jacobson, Victor 20
Jacques, Mrs. 19
James Bay 30, 47, 49, 50, 76, 102, 103, 143-145: bridge 49, 138, 143, 155; causeway 67, 104, 108, 127
Jenny Ford 47
Jewish Historical Society 82
Jewish people 80-82
Johnson Street ravine 9, 38, 49
Johnston, George 143
Kaiser Wilhelm 75
Kammerer, C.W. 59
Kane Street 122
Kane, Harriet Clench 120, 121
Kane, Paul 120-123
Kellett, Henry 25, 137
Kennedy, Arthur Edward 155
Kuper Avenue 24
Kuper Island 24

Index

Kuper, Augustus Leopold 22-24
Kurtz, John 51
Lady Head 20
Lady Lampson 20
Lama 124
Lampson Street 20
Laurel Point 34, 105, 138, 142
Laurier, Wilfrid 156, 157
Legislative Buildings 30, 46-47, 107
Lever Brothers 105
Loretto Hall 103-105
Lotbiniere Avenue 155, 156, 157
Lowe, Thomas 29
Macaulay Point 84, 94, 139
Macaulay, Donald 17, 19, 39, 193
Macdonald, William J. 29, 52
Maclure Street 114
Maclure, John 111
Maclure, Margaret Catherine Simpson "Daisy" 111, 112, 114
Maclure, Martha 111
Maclure, Samuel 111-114, 156
Marquis of Lorne 99
Mason, Jesse 148
Masonic Temple 53, 136, 145
Matsqui 111, 114
Maynard, Richard 139
McClure Street 115
McClure, Robert John LeMesurier 115
McFadden, R. 66
McGregor, J. Herrick 160
McInnes, Thomas 156
McKenzie, Kenneth 17
McLoughlin Point 139, 142
McLoughlin, John 139
McMicking Point 139
McMicking, Robert Burns 139
Mechanics Institute 100
Medana Street 146
Medana, Mary Helen 144
Medana, Paul 143-146
Medina, Paul. *See* Medana, Paul.
Medina's Grove 145-146
Memorial Crescent 76
Metchosin 139
Methodist Church 52-53, 65, 67, 98
Mill Bay 35
Miller, William 116
Mitchell, G. 66

Moresby Island 24
Moresby Park Terrace 24
Moresby Passage 24
Moresby Street 24
Moresby, Fairfax 22
Moresby, John 22-23, 24
Moses Point 139
Moses, Daniel David 139
Mouat, William Alexander 25
Mount Matheson 25
Mount St. Helen's 121
Munro Street 20
Munro, Alexander 20
Mystic Lane 97
Mystic Spring 95-97
The Mystic Spring and Other Tales of Western Life 96
Mystic Vale 97
Nagle, Captain 25
Nanaimo 14, 31, 33, 48, 84, 99, 152
Nesbitt, Jane Anne 36
Nesbitt, Samuel 36
New Westminster 26, 79, 82, 92-93, 111, 112, 114
Newcastle Island 14
Nootka Sound 29
North American Boundary Commission 86
North Saanich 139
North West Company 139
North West Territory. *See* Rupert's Land. *Northwest Digest* 136
Northwest Passage 115
"Oakdene" 44-45
Observatory Hill 132-133
Occidental Hotel 148-149
Ogden Point 139
Ogden, Peter Skene 14, 139
Old Burying Ground 38, 72, 85, 118, 145. *See also* Pioneer Square.
Old Cemeteries Society 165
Old Esquimalt Road 16-18, 21, 24, 71
Otter 25
Pandora 116
Pandora Street 40
Park Terrace 17
Paul Kane Place 120, 122
Pearkes, George W. 135
Pemberton, Joseph Despard 25, 46, 131, 155
Pendray Street 105
Pendray, Amelia Jane Carthew 102, 104-105
Pendray, Carl 102, 104

Pendray, Ernest 104
Pendray, Herbert 104
Pendray, Roy 104
Pendray, William Joseph 102-104
Pioneer Square 38, 145, 146. *See also* Old Burying Ground.
Ploughman of the Moon 162
Plumper 25
Plumper Bay 20
Point No Point 138, 141
Point Street 141
Pooley Place 94
Pooley, Charles Edward 92-94
Pooley, Charlie 93
Pooley, Elizabeth Wilhelmina Fisher 92-94
Pooley, Harry 93, 94
Pooley, Tom 93
Port Kuper 23, 24
post office 55, 63, 100, 124, 129
Powell River 44
Powell Street 42, 45
Powell, Israel Wood 42-45
Powell, Jennie Branks 43-45
Prince Albert of Saxe-Coburg and Gotha 139, 140
Princess Louise 32, 99
Princess Victoria 34
Prior Block 153
Prior Street 154
Prior, Edward Gawler 149, 151-154, 157
Prior, Genevieve Wright 153-154
Prior, Suzette Work 151, 153, 154
"The Priory" 151-152
Puget Sound Agricultural Company 16, 19, 20
Quadra 28
Queen Charlotte's Island 23
Queen Victoria 28, 30, 92, 99, 111, 135, 139, 140, 153
Queen's Market 64-67
Queensborough. *See* New Westminster.
Quimper, Manuel 16
R P Rithet 32
R.P. Rithet & Co. Ltd. 135
Race Passage Close 25
Race Rocks 25
Race Rocks lighthouse 25-27
Ragazzoni, J. 143
Rattenbury Place 106, 110
Rattenbury, Alma 109-110
Rattenbury, Florence 106, 109

Rattenbury, Francis Mawson 39, 100, 106-110, 113, 156
Rattenbury, Frank 110
Redfern Park 63
Redfern Street 63
Redfern, Alfred 61
Redfern, Alice 61
Redfern, Charles 5, 60-63, 67
Redfern, Eliza Arden Robinson 60-61, 63
Redfern, Elsie 61
Redfern, Harry 61
Redfern, Ina 61
Redfern, Kate 61
Redfern, Martha Eliza 61
Redfern, Will 61
Redfern, Winnifred 61
Reed, E. Baynes 127-128
Reminiscences of Old Victoria 97
Rhymes of a Rolling Stone 165
Richard Blanshard Building 68
Richards, George Henry 25
Riel Rebellion 159
Rithet, R.P. 30, 76
Robert Lowe 98
Robson, John 92, 94
Rock Bay Saw Mills 35-36
Rock Heights 17
Rocky Point 137
Roedde, Gustav 106
Ross Bay 128
Ross Bay Cemetery 146
Royal British Columbia Museum 89, 91
Royal Engineers 16, 26
Royal Hotel 32
Royal Roads 18, 27, 84, 139
Royal Roads University 114
Rudlin Bay 34
Rudlin Street 34
Rudlin, George 31-35
Rudlin, Sophia 32, 34
Rueffe, J. 147
Rupert's Land 76, 158
Sailor's Rest 20
Salish people 11
San Francisco 31
San Juan Islands 75, 76, 95
San Pedro 112
Sangster Lane 124
Sangster Plains 125

Index

Sangster, James 14, 124-126
Sangster, Mary 124, 125-126
Sapperton 26
Saskatchewan Legislative Buildings 159
Saw-se-a 122
Saxe Point 139, 140
Sayward Building 37
Sayward Farm 37
Sayward Road 37
Sayward Street 37
Sayward, Ann 36-37
Sayward, Joseph 36, 37
Sayward, William Parsons 35-37
Seabrook, Roads 135
Service Street 161
Service, Germaine Bourgoin 165
Service, Iris 165
Service, Robert William 161-165
Seymour, Frederick 88
Shah 27
Shakespeare Street 101
Shakespeare, Elizabeth 98, 99, 101
Shakespeare, Noah 5, 98-101, 153
Shakespeare, William 98
Shepard, Sam 35
Sheringham Point 140, 141
Sheringham, William Louis 140, 141
Shotbolt, Thomas 58
Signal Hill 19
Simpson, Aemilius 11
Simpson, George 11, 121
Simpson, May 19
Sims, William 144
Sinclair, John 12
Skinner, Thomas 17, 117
Smith, Alfred 132
Smith, Elizabeth 132
Smith, John 132
Smith, Philip 132
Somenos 161
Songhees Nation 11, 15, 21, 95
Songs of a Sourdough 165
Sooke 137, 141
Southgate, J.J. 52, 59
Spencer, David 53, 54, 67
Spencer, Emma 53
St John's Church 44
St. Andrew's Presbyterian Church 44
St. John's Anglican Church 61, 118, 135, 151

St. Paul's Anglican Church 19, 21
Stafford, John 64
Stevens, Al 66
Stoner, George Percy 110
Sunday School Association 100
Supreme Court of Vancouver Island 84
Swan, John 11
T.N. Hibben & Co. 58-59
Teague, John 151
telephone exchange 104, 139
Temple Building 112, 113
Ten Mile Point 142
Thetis 17, 22-24, 25
Thetis Cove 24
Thetis Crescent 24
Thetis Island 24
Thetis Lane 22, 24
Thumb Point 137
Tiedemann Creek/Glacier 48
Tiedemann Place 48
Tiedemann, Hermann Otto 9, 46-48, 50, 51, 107
Tiedemann, Mary Bissett 46, 47
Tiger Engine Company 71-72
Tolmie, Jane Work 151
Tolmie, William Fraser 43, 151
Topaze 17
The Trail of Ninety-eight 165
transatlantic cable 82
"Tregew" 50-51, 53
Trounce Alley 52-53, 54, 139
Trounce, Emma Richards 53
Trounce, Jane 49, 52
Trounce, Thomas 49-53
Trutch, Joseph 43, 90
Turner, Isabella 55
Turner, John 94
Tynemouth 60
Tyson, George 66
Una 124
University of British Columbia 44
Uplands Farm 13
Vancouver 34, 44, 106, 124
Vancouver Coal Mining and Land Company 151
Vancouver Island: colony of 42, 43, 58, 73, 74, 82, 83; HBC lease 16, 117; merged with British Columbia 64, 82, 85, 88, 90, 111; Confederation 28, 43-44, 112
Vancouver, George 29, 31
Venice 43

Victor Jacobson Park 20

Victoria 19, 28, 55, 62-63, 139: in late 1850s 35, 46, 49-50, 86, 143; in 1860s 8-9, 57, 70; in 1870s 102, 131; in 1889 144; in 1909 30; becomes city 21, 28, 57, 117; capital of B.C. 64, 82, 102; schools 43. *See also* Fort Victoria.

Victoria city hall 62, 64, 131, 136
Victoria Coffee and Spice Mills 148-149
Victoria District Church 9
Victoria Gazette 57, 125, 143
Victoria Harbour 13, 15, 30, 34, 46, 74, 76, 95, 137, 138, 139
Victoria jail 48, 51
Victoria Law Courts 9, 48, 51
Victoria Maritime Museum 9, 24, 48
Victoria Philharmonic Society 79, 80, 81
Victoria Times Colonist 115
Victoria Yacht Club 11, 137, 160
View Street 51, 59
Viewfield Farm 17, 19, 20, 93, 139
Virago 29
Volunteer Rifle Corps 118
W. & J. Wilson clothing store 54, 55-56
Waddington, Alfred 47, 57, 82
Waddington's Road 48
Walbran Island 30
Walbran Park 28, 30
Walbran Point 30
Walbran Rock 30
Walbran, Anne 30
Walbran, Florence 30
Walbran, John Thomas 28-31, 116, 129

Walkem, George Anthony 90
Wanderings of an Artist Among the Indians of North America 120, 122
Wee 39
Weiler Brothers 100
Weiler, John 52, 60
Western Slope 32
White Swan soap 102
Whitehorse 164
Wilson G Hunt 32
Wilson Street 56
Wilson, Elizabeth Eilbeck 54, 55-56
Wilson, Joseph 54-56
Wilson, Joseph E. 56
Wilson, Joseph Sr. 54, 55
Wilson, William 54-56, 60
"Woodvine Cottage" 36
Work Point 142
Work Point Barracks 21
Work, David 151
Work, John 21, 151
Work, Josette 151
Wright, John 81
Yarrow, Alfred 141
Yarrow, Norman 141
Yarrows Point 141
Yates Street 57, 147
YM/YWCA 100
Yosemite 32
Young Street 88
Young, Cecil 88
Young, Cecilia Eliza Cowan 83-84, 85, 86-87, 88
Young, William Alexander George 85, 86-88, 89

PHOTO CREDITS

British Columbia Archives: A-00278 (p. 12, b), A-04724 (p. 13), A-02707 (p. 14), PDP05443 (p. 17), F-07443 (p. 18), E-02700 (p. 20), I-61535 (p. 21), A-00271 (p. 23), E-03896 (p. 24), A-00535 (p. 26, l), C-05363 (p. 26, r), E-03803 (p. 27), A-02521 (p. 28), A-01983 (p. 29), PDP02240 (p. 31), A-00728 (p. 36), PDP00433 (p. 36, inset), F-00351 (p. 41, t), B-06132 (p. 43)), G-03969 (p. 45), G-02350 (p. 46, l), A-01698 (p. 46, r), A-01866 (p. 49, l), I-61534 (p. 49, r), A-08288 (p. 51), PDP03777 (p. 52), F-08557 (p. 53), F-05018 (p. 54, r), F-02887 (p. 57), A-03464 (p. 58), D-07713 (p. 61), E-01538 (p. 62), G-07944 (p. 64, l), G-07945 (p. 64, r), G-09095 (p. 69), A-05794 (p. 70), A-04790 (p. 71), H-03721 (p. 73, l), G-07855 (p. 73, r), F-06772 (p. 75), A-05567 (p. 77, r), PDP01782 (p. 78), A-02158 (p. 80), A-05964 (p. 81, t), C-08952 (p. 81, r), H-04961 (p. 83), A-01140 (p. 84), A-07029 (p. 86, l), A-09973 (p. 86, r), B-09328 (p. 87), C-06116 (p. 88, l), A-01752 (p. 88, r), A-07971 (p. 89), F-06182 (p. 90), G-08044 (p. 92), D-01847 (p. 93, l), G-05950 (p. 93, r), A-02977 (p. 96), H-03489 (p. 97), B-01413 (p. 98, l), G-04156 (p. 98, r), PDP01779 (p. 99), C-05468 (p. 100), C-06703 (p. 101), PDP00304 (p. 101, inset), C-06622 (p. 104), E-01894 (p. 107), D-08528 (p. 111, r), PDP00162 (p. 112), G-01052 (p. 116, l), G-01053 (p. 116, r), PDP01182 (p. 117), A-04988 (p. 118), A-04098 (p. 126), F-04522 (p. 128), F-08610 (p. 131), H-03543 (p. 133), A-01335 (p. 134, l), H-03432 (p. 134, r), A-02204 (p. 135, l), A-01333 (p. 135, r), PDP05420 (p. 138, b), E-04394 (p. 139), E-02206 (p. 140, t), I-20599 (p. 140, b), D-06203 (p. 142, t), H-00151 (p. 143), A-09210 (p. 144, b), A-02914 (p. 145), G-05189 (p. 147, r), C-08879 (p. 148), A-02706 (p. 149), A-04106 (p. 150), B-03365 (p. 151), D-07884 (p. 152), A-07478 (p. 154), I-46907 (p. 155), A-02821 (p. 156), PDP00327 (p. 158), D-06949 (p. 159), G-05117 (p. 160), G-03588 (p. 160, inset), F-02783 (p. 162), E-00235 (p. 163, b), F-06954 (p. 164)
John & Glenda Cheramy: pp. 8, 9, 12 (t), 33 (t), 41 (b), 48, 56, 63, 68, 74, 103 (b), 105 (t,b), 108 (t,b), 125, 130 (l), 138 (t), 141, 157
City of Victoria Archives: 98405-02-529 (p. 30), PR234-1664 (p. 32), PR252-7875 (p. 33, b), PR252-7872 (p. 34), 98109-02-4638 (p. 37), 98804-03-2470 (p. 39, l), PR35-3137 (p. 39, r), 96609-01-6351 (p. 40), 98803-20-7499 (p. 42), 96604-01-6491 (p. 44), PR254-881 (p. 50), PR60-5149 (p. 54, l), 98103-07-4114 (p. 55), 98302-02-04322 (p. 59), PR104-3428 (p. 60), 96604-01-1741 (p. 65), 96609-01-4133 (p. 66, t), 98312-07-3233 (p. 66, b), PR39-7464 (p. 67), PR252-6898 (p. 77, l), PR252-6900 (p. 79), PR234-1709 (103, t), PR35-800 (106, l), PR35-805 (106, r), PR35-815 (109), PR35-803 (110), PR127-3592 (111, l), 98410-10-764 (113), 98403-28-5075 (114), PR104-3383 (127), PR246-1131 (129), 96609-01-4132 (130, r), PR32-2497 (132), PR234-1667 (147, l), 96604-01-4109 (153, t), 98110-05-656 (153, b), 99008-01-3495 (163, t)
Robin Clarke: author photo
Heritage House collection: p. 47 and postcard images used on front and back cover, jacket flaps
Paul Kane V: p. 120
Royal Ontario Museum: pp. 122 (tl), 123 (b)
Saanich Archives: 1980-17-8 (142, b)
Stark Foundation, Orange, Texas: pp. 122 (tr, bl), 123 (t)
Vancouver Public Library: 9576 (p. 144, t)

THE AUTHOR

"Victoria's Favourite Street Walker"

Originally from Cheshire, England, Danda has lived in Canada since 1972 and on the West Coast since 1982. Her first career was nursing, then she qualified as a journalist, and over the years she has been an actor, broadcaster, public relations person, presentation skills coach, conference speaker, and last but not least, an historical storyteller and guide.

Danda arrived in Victoria in late 1996 and quickly noticed that its street names were different from those in other Canadian cities. Each intersection provided another opportunity to pause and ponder. Pretty soon she was getting a reputation for standing on street corners, so she "went underground," to libraries, archives, and pioneer societies, searching for the historic origins of Victoria's street names. A year later she submitted three articles to the *Times Colonist*…and a newspaper series was born.

Danda's habit of wandering along each street she writes about has earned her the unofficial title "Victoria's Favourite Street Walker." She is often joined by local residents and visitors, who are fascinated by the colourful characters who once lived here. Danda's special storytelling ability is enjoyed by all those who "step back in time" on her guided tours of Victoria's historic downtown, take one of her open-top bus tours through the city, gather for spooky stories in a cemetery, listen to her on the radio, or watch her on TV.

Danda's weekly column about the historic origin of street names first appeared in the *Victoria Times Colonist*'s "Islander" magazine in October 1977. Her first book, published in 1999, became one of the city's fastest selling regional titles in the past two decades. Her second book, published in 2000, quickly joined its predecessor on best-seller lists. You can reach Danda at: danda@dandahumphreys.com